GOLF AND GAUDÍ

GOLF AND GAUDÍ
The Golf Widow's Guide to Catalonia

by

Christopher Brown

Where to go, what to see, what to eat,
the history and culture of the region and
18 course descriptions for the golfer

The Pentland Press Limited
Edinburgh · Cambridge · Durham · USA

© Christopher Brown 1999

First published in 1999 by
The Pentland Press Ltd.
1 Hutton Close
South Church
Bishop Auckland
Durham

British Library Cataloguing in Publication Data.
A catalogue record for this book is available
from the British Library.

ISBN 1 85821 713 X

Typeset by George Wishart & Associates, Whitley Bay.
Printed and bound by Antony Rowe Ltd., Chippenham.

For Peter and Marianne,
two golfing friends who have shown
such courage in adversity.

Contents

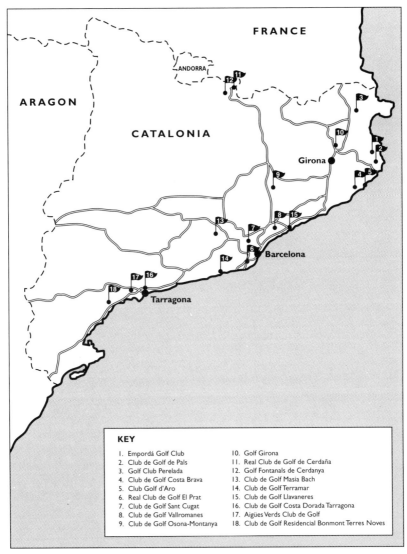

KEY

1. Empordá Golf Club
2. Club de Golf de Pals
3. Golf Club Perelada
4. Club de Golf Costa Brava
5. Club Golf d'Aro
6. Real Club de Golf El Prat
7. Club de Golf Sant Cugat
8. Club de Golf Vallromanes
9. Club de Golf Osona-Montanya
10. Golf Girona
11. Real Club de Golf de Cerdaña
12. Golf Fontanals de Cerdanya
13. Club de Golf Masia Bach
14. Club de Golf Terramar
15. Club de Golf Llavaneres
16. Club de Golf Costa Dorada Tarragona
17. Aigües Verds Club de Golf
18. Club de Golf Residencial Bonmont Terres Noves

Location of courses described in this book.

Foreword

This book is written for and addressed to the unsung heroine of the world of golf, the golfer's ever-patient, selfless, non-golfing wife. She always asks him, 'How did you play, dear?' when he returns from his weekend game even though she already knows this from the sound of his car door slamming shut, and then listens to the usual saga of missed putts and unlucky breaks. She still occasionally wonders how mature and intelligent – well, more or less – adults, many of whom earn their bread tussling with the all-too-real problems of the business world, can become so infatuated with the inconsequential game of golf but she accepts it, happy that he enjoys it, which is a good enough reason for her. I always think of Bing Crosby's wife in this respect: she described her husband as a golfer who could sing.

This is in a sense a travel book, describing the history, culture and gastronomy of this corner of Europe as well as explaining what the non-golfer can do and see in each location, and its format, with a detailed Table of Contents and Appendices for quick reference, should make it a practical guide to take with you.

It is also a book for golfers and golfing couples, particularly those who enjoy playing new courses while on vacation but not to the exclusion of mixing some cultural sorties with their sport, and who also enjoy good food and wine. Some golfing travellers want nothing more than to play golf every day and lie on their backs in the sun after their round. For these, the course descriptions will, I hope, fire up their enthusiasm on a winter's evening to make their next golfing pilgrimage to Catalonia, where the choice of venue is extensive and the scenery everything from mountain to coastal Mediterranean. All distances given off the tees are from the yellow tees – the members' tees – and the comments on the individual holes on a specific course are those of a sexagenarian eleven-handicapper so they will not be much of a guide to the low-handicap player. The reader who would prefer being spared the experience of plowing through the course descriptions just has to look for the symbol ꓘ ꓘ ꓘ which marks the end of the details of a particular course.

The order in which the different districts and their courses are described follows no special logic but is written on the assumption that the visitor will have a car available. Some notable Catalan beauty spots do not feature in this book simply because there is no golf course near them and, similarly, ideal beaches and coastal areas are outside its scope although if you have small children with you it would make sense to choose the courses close to the coast. Inevitably, one of the hardest tasks which an author of a book of this kind has to face is just what to include from such a richness of subject matter available.

The names of towns, streets and buildings are mostly written in Catalan because that is how they appear on signposts and town guides, and for the same reason the names of different dishes are also in Catalan although their equivalents in English and Spanish are given in Appendix 1.

Originally, I intended not recommending individual restaurants and hotels because they are subject to rapid change in quality if the establishment changes hands. However, as I have almost always benefited from such recommendations from friends if visiting an area for the first time, when you usually come off much better than if you just take pot luck, I decided to include some because these, up to the time of writing, are a few whose standards and quality I have always enjoyed. Not included are two and three star Michelin Guide establishments, of which there are several in Catalonia; for those readers interested in eating in them the Michelin Guide for Spain and Portugal is available in most book shops in the region and will cost you less than the tip for the meal.

An alternative to staying in hotels is to use farmhouses in and around the villages. Rural tourism is now quite a big part of Spain's tourist industry, and the regional government's Tourist Authority has published a comprehensive guide to rural accommodation, '*Guia de Residencies – casa de Pagès*'. I have not included any here, partly because they are sometimes more expensive than an adequate hotel and do not have many of its services, and also because I have no personal experience of them. If this option does appeal to you, your travel agent should be able to obtain a copy of the guide.

For the reader who would like to delve deeper into Catalan history, customs, culture and idiosyncrasies Robert Hughes' excellent, encyclopaedic and very readable book 'Barcelona' (Harvill Harper Collins) could be the next step.

Finally, I hope that my Catalan friends who read this book will do so with the patient resignation that the golfers among them would show to a foursomes partner who keeps hitting his shots out-of-bounds.

Sant Andreu de Llavaneres
March 1999

An Introduction to Catalonia

Catalonia is one of those regions in Europe which have pronounced individual characters, usually because they were once nation-states and sometimes, as is the case here, even have their own language. It is a triangular wedge of territory forming the north-east corner of the Iberian peninsula and so, today, part of Spain. Stretching four hundred kilometres from the French border on the Mediterranean coast down to just south of the town of Sant Carles de la Rapita and, at its widest point, running inland along the Pyrenees just over two hundred kilometres as the crow flies, the region covers an area of 32,106 square kilometres, slightly larger than Belgium, and almost a third of it lies in the Pyrenees. The population today is over six million, half of whom live in the Barcelona metropolitan area, and their income per capita is almost thirty percent higher than the average for Spain. Catalonia is also Spain's principal industrial region, accounting for twenty percent of the country's gross domestic product with only fifteen percent of the total population. Those are the bare statistics but the attractions of the region have nothing to do with numbers, leaving aside for the moment the question of golf scores, and very much to do with scenery, history, the arts and architecture, and, not least, good food and wine at reasonable prices. To these must be added the climate, which is everything from mountain to Mediterranean coastal. It is a very attractive destination for the traveller with broad, cultural interests or who relishes driving through glorious countryside, or who simply enjoys lounging on a beach. And for the golfer, it offers year-round golf on most of its thirty one courses in what must be close to the ideal climate for the game, neither exhaustingly hot and humid in the summer months nor at all cold in winter on the coastal strip, and with low rainfall.

The region is divided for administrative purposes into four provinces, Barcelona, Girona, Tarragona and Lleida, and is further subdivided into forty one small districts, called *comarques* in Catalan, which are much in evidence as you drive around because the regional government has placed signs at the roadside giving you a brief idea of what to expect wherever you cross into a new district. These *comarques* go back as far as 1588 and so are very much a part of Catalan life.

A short historical perspective

To understand and enjoy the essence of Catalonia, the people, customs and the artistic, literary and architectural heritage so evident wherever you go, a look at the region's history is a prerequisite.

Before this century the usual thesis of historians was that civilization in Spain started with the arrival of Greek colonists at Empúries on the Costa Brava in the sixth century BC but that their civilizing influence never spread very far into the Iberian peninsula, so that it was not until the arrival of the Romans at the end of the second century BC that this corner of the Mediterranean benefited from the influence of a superior culture. However, some major archaeological finds during the last ninety years or so have revealed that the Iberos, the tribes inhabiting all of the Mediterranean fringe from Adge in the Languedoc region of France down to southern Andalucia between the seventh and first centuries BC, developed a structured society, with an aristocratic warrior class and even well organized urban communities, and they left many examples of a surprisingly sophisticated culture. They had their own writing, which has still not been deciphered although the words for bench, beer and shovel are known, as is a common insult *gurdus*, meaning stupid, which is one you could let slip at the golfer in moments of frustration. But it is the stunningly beautiful sculptures, jewellery, ceramics and bronze castings which, above all, reveal the degree of refinement of their society. If you ever coincide with an exhibition of Ibero culture do not miss it.

It was, however, the Romans who put an indelible imprint on all of Iberia and particularly Catalonia, erasing in the course of time everything that had gone before and bequeathing the nucleus of almost everything that followed, from language and construction techniques to art and religion. Only the Moorish influence would later distinguish Spanish culture from those deriving from the Romans in the other European Latin countries. The Romans, who founded Barcelona and Tarragona, which under them was the capital of northern Iberia, stayed in Catalonia until the arrival of the Visigoths, Germanic tribes from the north, at the end of the fourth century, who remained for three hundred years but left little evidence of their occupation. The Moors arrived in Catalonia in 717 and held sway over the region until 803 when Louis the Pious, king of Aquitaine and the son of Charlemagne, ousted them from Barcelona and all the territory north to the Pyrenees, what would later be known as *Catalunya Vella* – Old Catalonia, although the Moors still controlled the land to the south, *Catalunya Nova* – New Catalonia, and did not completely abandon Catalan territory for another two hundred years.

With the arrival of the French *Catalunya Vella* became part of the Carolingian empire and was to depend on the emperors for defence against the Moors for almost the next three hundred years. It was the Hispanic Marches to the French, an area of widely differing terrain consisting of fiefdoms ruled by a local count or baron, who lived off the peasant farmers through punitive taxes in return for defending the county against outsiders. Scraps between one count and another were constant in a struggle to gain territorial advantage, and and it was one such warrior with the memorable name of Guifré el Pilós, Wilfred the Hairy, who carved himself a way with his sword to a position of dominance in the second half of the ninth century, and in so doing established Barcelona for good as the capital of the region. The exact date of his birth is not known but he died around 898, revered since by Catalans as the founder of the Catalan nation. He achieved control of *Catalunya Vella* ultimately at the expense of the French regent, who was under something of cloud at the emperor's court and therefore his demise was without political risk for the usurper who was careful to recognize his loyalty to the Carolingian emperor until his death. He was the first of the Catalan counts of Barcelona and the last to be invested with his title by the emperor. Henceforth, his descendants would inherit the title automatically and after the failure of the French to come to their aid when Al-Mansur, the Vizier of Cordoba, retook Barcelona in 985, Catalonia became effectively an independent state.

Guifré el Pilós established a united Catalonia but crediting him also with creating the Catalan flag, *la Senyera* as it is called, is more than questionable. The myth surrounding this affair relates that Louis the Pious, aided in the battle with the Saracens during the siege of Barcelona by Guifré el Pilós, who was wounded in the fighting, came to Guifré's tent and as a mark of gratitude awarded him a new coat of arms by dipping his fingers in Guifré's blood and drawing four crimson lines down his gold-coloured shield, which equates with the design and colours of the Catalan flag. Unfortunately, historical events belie this: both the conquest of Barcelona from the Moors and Louis' death occurred before Guifré was born. Still, it's a nice story to tell the children although the fact is the origins of the Catalan flag are not known.

One altruistic attribute that features large in the life of Guifré was his generosity in the founding of churches and monasteries, and in so doing he not only launched one of the jewels of Catalan artistic endeavour, Romanesque architecture, on its scintillating way but also set the pattern by granting land and funds to the Church that future kings and nobles would follow for the next four centuries. As a result, Catalonia is the largest repository of Romanesque architecture and art in Europe today. The importance of the Church in Catalan society would, with one or two anticlerical hiccups on the way, remain undiminished until the nineteenth century. The clergy together with the nobility were the educated class in the Middle Ages in Spain, the intelligentsia of the time and the source of all academic growth and improvement. They were the brains of mediaeval society and a dominant influence on it, and were, apart from the defensive fortresses built by the local nobles to defend their territory, the beneficiaries of each generation's most important construction projects – churches, cathedrals and monasteries.

Mediaeval Catalonia was a feudal society with an aristocratic class dominating the peasants and serfs under them. As in France, the nobility formed a complex hierarchy, what was known elsewhere as the Order of Chivalry, with the nobles of oldest lineage at the top, owners of large estates and numerous castles, down to the lower levels whose sphere of action was only local. However chivalrous they may have been, this did not stop them from ruthlessly exploiting the peasants and even seizing their smallholdings, apart from grinding rapacious taxes out of them. The count-kings of Barcelona were the only brake on this abuse, and it was Ramon Berenguer I who, around 1068, took the revolutionary step in a European context of codifying a Bill of Rights, *Les Usatges*, to defend the interests of all the classes in Catalan society. Fundamentally, it established that 'worthy citizens', which meant anyone above the level of a serf, had equal rights before the law with the nobility, and that in cases of dispute these had to be settled by an arbitrator. Thus, Catalonia became the first country in Europe to have a Bill of Rights, more than a hundred years before England got its Magna Carta.

In 1137, Count Berenguer IV married Princess Petronila of Aragón and this converted the Countship of Barcelona into the Kingdom of Catalonia and Aragón, and launched Catalonia on the most splendid period of its history and Barcelona on a wave of commercial growth and prosperity which has rarely been matched since. By the thirteenth century, the momentum of Catalan expansion was so great that, almost inevitably, within the body of its imperial growth the virus of its future decline was already developing. Between 1229, when Jaume I sailed to dislodge the Moors from Mallorca, and 1324, when his great-grandson conquered Sardinia, the Catalan empire became dominant in the northern Mediterranean, having also acquired by conquest Valencia, Ibiza, Sicily and Menorca. The conquest of Sicily led to the taking of the dukedoms of Athens and Neopatria, and the commercial interests of Catalonia-Aragon were assured by the establishment of consulates in Syria, Egypt, Malta and the Adriatic, and in the fifteenth century even Naples became part of the empire.

What was to be a gradual but eventually terminal decline in the fortunes of Catalonia as an independent kingdom began when Ferdinand II of Aragón succeeded to the throne of Aragón and Catalonia in 1452 because it was he who married Isabella of Castilla, thus uniting the destinies of Catalonia with those of central Spain. Once married, the *Reyes Catolicos*, the Catholic Monarchs as they were to be labelled by history, moved the court out of Barcelona and henceforth the Crown would be represented in Catalonia by a Viceroy, known as *El Lugarteniente*. Finally, in 1714 all Catalan pretence of political independence from Spain was wiped out at the end of the Spanish War of Succession, when Philip V's troops ended their siege of Barcelona, started because the Catalan government had backed the other pretender to the Spanish throne, the Archduke of Austria, by taking the city in a final assault on 11 September. Within days the annulment of Catalonia's 400-year-old political institutions had been decreed and the most traumatic event in Catalan history consummated.

Since then an undercurrent of almost pathological distrust has run between Madrid, meaning everything from central government to the trivia of rival, sporting endeavours, and Barcelona, meaning Catalonia, fuelled by suspicion on the part of Madrid that Catalonia would always seek its independence again and by resentment in Catalonia that their ancient independence and political institutions had been taken away from them by the force of arms. Only after the death of Franco and the reorganization of Spain under a new constitution in 1978 into self-governing autonomous regions, which was endorsed by a large majority in a national referendum with the Catalan vote also strongly in favour, have the demons of this historic animosity been, apparently, put to flight.

The Catalan language
Catalan is a Romance language and therefore a direct derivation of the vulgar Latin spoken in this part of the Iberian peninsula during and after the Roman occupation. That it is spoken today in the south-west corner of France, the Balearic islands, the region of Valencia, Andorra and some towns in Corsica is a consequence of the territorial expansion of Catalonia in the thirteenth and fourteenth centuries, whose conquering kings replaced the Moors resident in these territories with colonists from Catalonia. As early as the ninth century Catalan words appear in otherwise Latin documents but it was in the twelfth century that the first documents were written entirely in Catalan, the oldest known of which is the *Homilies d'Organya*, meaning, roughly, sermons on biblical texts.

It was Ramon Llull in the thirteenth century who established, single-handed, Catalan as a literary language, with some 256 texts in Catalan, Latin and Arabic to his credit. This extraordinary personality, part scholar, mystic, philosopher and missionary, was born in Palma de Mallorca but at the age of thirty he abandoned his material possessions and his wife and family to set off on a fifty-year mission aimed at convincing the Islamic world by reasoned argument alone of the superiority of Christianity, so he deserves to be labelled a hopeless optimist as well. His travels included Paris, Rome and Genoa as well as Egypt, Libya and parts of Asia Minor, and his life's literary output exceeded 27,000 pages! Since his time, there has been a rich roll-call of literary names down the centuries establishing a solid corpus of poetry and prose in Catalan.

Catalonia under Franco lived through one of its more miserable periods as a proud, historic region with its own, clear differential in culture and language, both of which suffered severe repression under the regime to the extent that the Catalan language was not allowed to be taught in the schools or universities, so that the majority of the generation of Catalans who were educated between 1939 and 1976 are scarcely literate in their mother tongue. After Franco they made up for it, though, with everything displayed in public written in Catalan and even to the extent that the Castillian-speaking children of Spaniards from other regions resident in Catalonia are virtually obliged to acquire their education in Catalan, like it or not. And if a university student from another country wants to study in a Catalan university he will have to be prepared to take all his instruction in Catalan although he can present his written work in Spanish.

Today, Catalan is spoken by more than six million people as their first language, more than Danish or Norwegian for example, and together with Spanish, Gallego (spoken in Galicia), and the Basque language, is one of the four official languages of Spain. There are two TV channels and several radio stations which broadcast exclusively in Catalan, and currently two daily newspapers in the language. You will have to cope with some Catalan during your visit – on road signs, menus, place-names and simple instructions like 'push' or 'pull' on doors and which of the rest rooms is yours. However, all Catalans speak Spanish so if you can speak it they will always converse with you in '*Castellano*', to give it its correct name.

Romanesque art and buildings

Almost all the districts of Catalonia have a wealth of Romanesque churches, particularly so in the Pyrenees where the Saracen invaders never made more than temporary incursions into the northern valleys and so the churches were left intact. This architectural period, which in Catalonia lasted from the eleventh to the end of the fourteenth century, is a major historical element in Catalan culture although its early period, called Lombard Romanesque, received its inspiration from northern Italy as the name suggests. It was a new architectural style following on what had previously been Byzantine from the eastern part of the Roman Empire, and was called Romanesque because its buildings looked much like Roman buildings; they were built to last, too, with a large number of them still in use today. When you want to visit a Romanesque church in a village you just have to go to the Town Hall, the *Ajuntament*, and ask for the key.

As you drive round the countryside small isolated Romanesque chapels, usually referred to as hermitages in Catalonia, pop out at you in quite unexpected places, built no doubt by some pious nobleman to mark a major occurrence in his life, and still a pleasant reminder to the traveller of an age when, in spite of the crude harshness of most people's existence, the faith was the source of spiritual solace for the majority.

Romanesque art had two principal branches: wooden carvings and paintings, most of which are murals in churches. To see both you should visit the *Museu Nacional d'Art de Catalunya* (MNAC) in Barcelona, where a magnificent collection of carvings and, above all, murals is displayed. The murals have been removed from their original churches using a special technique developed for the purpose and they are displayed in life-size models of each original church. This was done to preserve them from further degradation due to the unsuitable ambiental conditions in old and humid churches. The Episcopal museum in Vic also has an excellent collection of Romanesque carvings.

That Romanesque art was to have a lasting influence on painting even to the present day is a mark of its significance. Robert Hughes, the author and art critic, recounts how Joan Miró (1893-1983), whom he calls Catalonia's greatest painter since the twelfth century, spent hours every year studying Romanesque art in the museum which today is the MNAC. A visit to Catalonia would not be complete without spending some time looking at this rich legacy from the Middle Ages.

Architecture and the arts in Catalonia

As you would expect in a region with a two-thousand-year history, a rich collection of architectural styles greets you wherever you go. Romanesque was followed by Gothic, and there are outstanding examples of this architectural period in the cathedrals in the four provincial capitals of Girona, Barcelona, Tarragona and Lleida, while fine Gothic churches can be visited in most of the region's small towns. The *Barrio Gotico* – the Gothic Quarter – in Barcelona and the old part of Girona have marvellous collections of buildings from this period, entire streets which have remained unchanged since they were built apart from the paving of roads, and the atmosphere as you meander along them can, if your mood is right, be time-warping.

The Moderniste movement in architecture, which is very much a distinguishing feature of Barcelona although there are examples of the style all over Catalonia, began in the 1880s and lasted until about 1910, and it includes Gaudí's unfinished Basilica of the Sacred Family, famous

Joan Miró. Arxiu històric, Ajuntament de Barcelona.

9

the world over, not least in Japan from where substantial funds have
come to enable construction to continue. Some time must be spent
during a stay in the region's capital experiencing the visual pleasure to
be had from these buildings which are enormously varied and
entertaining, and the tourist is well catered for by organized guided
tours provided by the city authorities.

Noucentisme was the movement which followed Modernisme, and it
was a reaction against the romantic extravaganzas of Modernisme. This
new artistic movement was inspired originally by a novel by Eugeni
d'Ors, *La Ben Plantada*, published in 1912 and evoking the ground roots
of the Mediterranean man and the timeless heritage accumulated since
Roman times. In architecture it was a reversion to Classicism, not least
that of the type seen in bank buildings, and it would hold sway for the
next two decades but it is difficult to imagine that it will ever excite
future generations' interest in the way Modernisme does today.

Since the Middle Ages art has always been an important part of the
Catalan cultural scene. The cathedrals and churches are full of
extraordinarily detailed and stylized altar-pieces from all periods, and
sculptors could always earn their bread in church construction even in
Gaudí's day. Painting had a jump-start with Romanesque but the
prolificity did not end in the fourteenth century even if what was to
come was not in the same league as Velazquez, Goya, Murillo and
Zurbarán. Jaume Huguet is considered one of the best Spanish painters
of the fifteenth century, and Antonio Viladomat continued the tradition
in the eighteenth. The nineteenth century witnessed a surge of gifted
artists, names like Martí Alsina, J. Vayreda, Fortuny, Rusiñol and Ramon
Casas, and, of course, Picasso, who was a native of Malaga but spent
some of his formative years as a young man painting in Barcelona and
playing a prominent part in a group of bohemian painters' social life at
the end of the century prior to leaving for Paris. He later donated
numerous paintings to the city, which can be seen in the Picasso
museum. The twentieth century produced two Catalans who were
international giants of modern art – Dalí and Miró. Joan Miró was a
quiet, introspective little man with a galaxy of talent; Salvador Dalí was
arguably the period's painter with the biggest ego, a theatrical extrovert
whose week would not have been complete without some outrageous
antics to attract the media. Because he lived much of his life in Catalonia
in the district of the Alt Empordà the pleasure of delving into the

domestic details of his day-to-day existence can be indulged at two of his homes now open to the public.

Today, Barcelona has become something of a magnet for young painters from all over the world, much like Paris has always been, and the number of art museums and galleries must make it one of the largest of such offerings in Europe. Contemporary artists from Barcelona with well-established international reputations include Tápies and Miquel Barceló.

Gastronomy

Man, particularly the golfing variety, cannot live for long on the fruits of the arts alone so he, and probably you too, will enjoy a trip to a region which knows how to cook and has all the classical Mediterranean ingredients to ensure a very varied cuisine. With a long coastline it is not surprising that fish takes pride of place over meat, and its freshness results from the proximity of most of the territory to a local port so that the day's catch is typically auctioned and in a fishmonger's shop within a couple of hours after it was landed, and you have only to watch the fishing boats off-loading a day's catch to appreciate the wide variety on offer.

Fruit and vegetables are also staples of the Mediterranean diet and again they are invariably day-fresh. Local residents are spoilt in being able to buy their produce at a local market knowing that it was pulled out of the ground or off the tree no more than twelve hours previously, and that degree of freshness does wonders for the flavour and texture of whatever you eat. All of this translates into a usually huge choice in any restaurant, which can be bewildering to those not yet familiar with just what a given dish will actually turn out to be, and often the English translation, if there is one, leaves you little wiser. So be adventurous and try anything that sounds interesting, particularly if it is one of the house specialities.

Wine is produced virtually all over Catalonia and there are eight different zones which have regulatory bodies guaranteeing that the wines produced there are made only with grapes from the area and that other parameters in the production and maturing of the wines meet required standards. In Spain these quality wines from a specific area are labelled as D.0., *denominación de origen*. Catalonia has always been considered one of the best regions in Spain for white wines and specially champagne, called *cava* for trademark reasons. Today, however, excellent red wines are also produced and the trend is to improve quality and consequently increase the price. All restaurants offer house wines and these are almost always quite acceptable; they are also required by law to offer a fixed price menu, which, if you are concerned about how much a meal may cost you, is an effective control on the total cost. If you choose to picnic at mid-day it makes sense to visit the local wine store and buy a litre (or whatever quantity you require) of whatever takes your fancy from the vat, and they will always let you sample several before choosing. Wines sold in bulk start as low as Ptas 135 per litre, and for Ptas 160 or so you can buy a very drinkable *vi*, vino in Catalan.

The countryside
Josep Pla (1897-1981) is the writer who first revealed the soul and his own consummate love of this region in his books *Catalunya* and *Costa Brava* but unless your Spanish is up to scratch or Catalan makes light reading for you – Pla wrote in both – the brief descriptions in this book will, probably inadequately, have to be your guide on what awaits you if you visit. Pla said almost apologetically that whatever the reader might think about the Catalan countryside he would at least have to admit that it offers some spectacular panoramas, and this is undeniable. Like most places on earth, especially in the industrialized countries, there are areas of the bleakest horrors of what man can do to destroy whatever nature has created, from industrial wastelands and blighted beaches to simply insensitive if not downright irresponsible construction destroying otherwise paradisal countryside, and there are industrial nightmare areas to rival any other in Europe. But once away from these Catalonia has a variety of wonderful scenery within its confines that few other regions of similar size in Europe can match.

For mountain scenery the area within the foothills and mountains of the Pyrenees is all that you would expect from a mountain environment. Just how rural you want to be will decide how far into the mountain valleys you go but wherever that is in these mountains will prove gratifyingly natural and unspoilt unless, of course, you choose a bustling ski resort.

Catalonia's Costa Brava hardly needs a boost here, being probably one of the best known of the popular stretches of coast on the

Mediterranean. Technically the Costa Brava starts at the French border and reaches down to the town of Blanes, and people who know it well all have their favourite stretch. There are some over-developed beaches backed by high-rise monstrosities but away from these there are hundreds of small coves with the pines growing almost to the water's edge, and the clarity of the sea is another hallmark of this coast. The nineteenth-century Catalan poet, Joan Maragall, captured something of the effect the beauty of the Costa Brava scenery can have on the viewer in these lines:

> *Dues coses hi ha*
> *que el mirar-les juntes*
> *em fan el cor més gran:*
> *la verdor dels pins*
> *la blavor del mar.*

> There are two things
> which seen together
> make my heart swell:
> the verdancy of the pines
> the blueness of the sea.

South of the Costa Brava the beaches continue almost without interruption to Sant Carles de la Rapita but the scenery is not the same and the water, although warmer, is not as transparent, which does not in any way mean that they should be avoided because they attract as many, if not more, bathers than the Costa Brava.

The further south you go, and the first perceptible change is apparent even at Sitges, the countryside takes on a drier look, accentuated by acres of vineyards interspersed with almond and olive trees, and with a sierra usually forming the horizon inland. It is quite unlike the densely-forested terrain that stretches to the west of Girona and up to the Pyrenees. But such is the typical Mediterranean mix of high mountains, large, heavily-cultivated plains and thick forests, all ringed at the perimeter by this ancient, magical sea.

The modern Catalan

It is both a blessing and a curse that modern technology, particularly in communications, is fast ironing out the differences in character and customs between nations. That educational standards and programmes in the developed world are virtually the same everywhere inevitably makes for a more universal citizen, who furthermore lives any drama from your country on his evening TV news just as you do. The benefits are obvious: the differences in living standards decrease and the historical prejudices felt towards aliens lose all relevance when the foreigner thinks, reacts and even laughs at much the same things as you. The downside is that the developed world is losing much of the spice of variety between one country and another.

Catalans today, as a whole, are very much like anyone else. This is not to say that their traditional virtues of hard work, down-to-earth common sense – *seny* – and a well developed degree of caution in spending their money are no longer there: jokes about tight-fisted Catalans are still told with relish in Catalonia and the rest of Spain. In many ways they are not unlike the traditional Yorkshireman – someone who quickly labels a free spender as having more money than sense, believes in calling a spade a spade, distrusts anyone who puts on airs and graces, and is not renowned for being a spontaneous bundle of fun.

On first acquaintance they can be reserved, unlike the outgoing Madrileño, but then so are many people in most countries. The family, as in all of Spain, is the most important priority throughout their lives and much of social life revolves round family reunions. In business they are pragmatists and usually skilled negotiators, and in modern politics, at least, tireless beavers nibbling away at the central government in Madrid to obtain additional power for their regional government. Like all Spaniards they are unfailingly courteous and welcome the foreign visitor with genuine enthusiasm, delighted that Catalonia is the chosen vacation destination and proud to show off its treasures.

Golf in Catalonia

The oldest course in the region was founded by English residents living in Barcelona in 1914 but the growth of a sport that requires an abundant supply of water in this climate and substantial tracts of land was scarcely measurable in the following thirty one years: by 1945 there were still only three clubs. The spurt in golf course construction began in the sixties, and today there are thirty one courses in Catalonia, not a large number by American or British standards but pretty decent in a continental European context.

Golf is a highly structured sport in Spain, as are most sports. All clubs belong to a regional Golf Federation, which is a branch of the Spanish Golf Federation based in Madrid, and these bodies administer all aspects of the game from running the handicap system to organizing official golf tournaments and liaising with equivalent organizations in other countries. To play in competitions in Spain you must have a Spanish Federation licence, which costs Ptas 6,000 per year. Membership fees at clubs obviously vary but most clubs charge between Ptas 10,000 and 20,000 per month. The differences in green fees are more pronounced and are usually higher at the weekends; in Appendix II current green fees for the courses described in this book are listed together with other essential details.

Some clubs will ask a visitor to show some proof that he has an official handicap in his home country before letting him out on the course so at least a letter avowing this from your club secretary would be useful to bring with you. More and more clubs in the region do not allow metal spiked golf shoes.

Seniors golf is also well organized and dynamically managed. Ladies over fifty and men over fifty five are eligible, and for the Ptas 10,000 annual fee which is paid to AESGOLF, the Spanish Seniors Golf Association, who also require you to have the Federation licence, the member can play in any Seniors event anywhere in Spain. For those eligible and who are in the country for sufficient time each year it is excellent value for money because in Seniors competitions, which are always played on weekdays, you pay no green fee and the entrance fee for a one-day competition is typically only Ptas 1,500. The Seniors in Catalonia also get up to fifty per cent discount off green fees at many clubs on weekdays. Most of the regions in Spain have a large programme of Senior events each year.

Some courses have favourable green fees for guests at certain hotels in their area; the only way to check this is to contact the clubs you are interested in playing for details of such hotels. Similarly, groups may be able to negotiate more favourable green fees at some clubs. Reserving start times varies from one club to another so it pays to call the course you want to play a day or two before to see if you can reserve your start time. One of the big bonuses of playing the Catalan courses is that they are seldom overcrowded with visitors on weekdays, unlike so many courses on the Costa del Sol or in Mallorca.

Average, maximum shade temperatures in the summer months are usually between 27° and 32°C, and in winter on the coastal strip the average maximum is between 12° and 15°C. The humidity in summer is variable but rarely oppressive. Inland courses in winter are sometimes subject to a light ground frost at night but by about 11 a.m. the sun has thawed this out. The autumn is perhaps the best time of year for golf in terms of temperature but it is also subject to occasional heavy rainstorms which are usually tropical in intensity but brief.

Whether you come to Catalonia for the golf or to enjoy all the other good things this region has to offer you can be confident that you will return home at the end of your visit replete with gratifying memories of your Catalan adventure and maybe even one or two phrases in Catalan – *Bon dia! Moltes gracies!* and, most importantly because it means you will be coming back, *A reveure!*

II

The District of L'Empordà

Empordà Golf Club

Opened in 1991 with twenty seven holes, leaving another nine still to be built, this course was quickly recognized as a landmark in Catalan golf. Designed by Robert van Hagge Design Associates and built on land forming part of the delta of the river Ter, Empordà Golf Club was a new concept in golf course design, at least in this corner of the world. The surrounding area is completely flat, marshy land where rice is still cultivated, and the land the course was built on was previously rice fields. The first nine holes have many of the characteristics of a links course but with a large number of water hazards added; the fairways are rarely flat, replete with mounds and hollows and with small hummocks, similar in size and shape to sand dunes defining their borders and the rough appears to be genuine links grass, long, wiry and often very penalizing. The second nine are more Mediterranean in character, their fairways lined with tall pine trees with a few acacias interspersed among them, and water is much in play on several holes. All the greens are very fast and full of breaks.

Voted by the readers of one of Spain's leading golf magazines as one of the ten best courses in the country, Empordà is just what you would like to find in any layout deserving the accolade of an outstanding course. It is very testing but fair, free of artificially created difficulties that penalize what is a good shot for an average-handicap golfer, such as trees planted or left standing in the middle of fairways, and at 5,855 metres (6,403 yards) for a par of seventy one it's also long. For the low-handicapper there are holes that offer two options off the tee, one adventurous and the other cautious, with dire penalties for the brave if they go astray, while the average player can finish at net par if he strikes the ball consistently well and straight, can read the greens correctly and can keep his nerve playing to those greens which are tightly protected by water. Wayward shots are always penalized one way or another.

Water is in play on twelve holes and it is there to welcome your Parmaker at the first tee on the Llevant course but only if he pulls his drive well to the left after lining it up on the mediaeval Tower of the Hours in Pals, clearly visible some five kilometres distant. The second hole offers the temptation for the longer hitter to drive over the water leaving a short pitch shot, while the less endowed play to the right of the hazard leaving themselves a mid-iron to a generously sized green.

As you stand on the third tee take a moment to look at the outline of the hills to the north to see the shape of a recumbent bishop wearing his mitre and with his hands clasped over his chest, his bishop's ring clearly evident (it is, in fact, the castle of Montgri), and endowed with a paunch worthy of a senior prelate, followed by long legs leading to his feet way over to the right of your view.

The short par four fourth requires pin-point accuracy on the shot to a green protected by bunkers to the left and water on the right which extends round behind the putting surface. The par three sixth, 159 metres (174 yards), has a huge bunker extending all the way from the tee to the green which helps to concentrate the mind wondrously. The 531 metres (582 yards) eighth is the number 1 stroke index hole, which is unusual in a par five but the first-time visitor will soon learn why, apart from its length, when he plays it. He can dump his drive into water in three different ways: to the left, to the right and by hitting it straight but too far! If he is still dry thus far he is now faced with a second over more water, followed by a longish third which will find a long bunker to the right of the fairway if he imparts even a hint of a slice to the shot. Finally, the green itself has some subtle little breaks in it so it is easy to three-putt.

Relieved to have the eighth behind him, the visitor faces more peril on the ninth, rated the three handicap hole and running 348 metres (381 yards). If he pulls his drive he is in water again so he should play to the right hand side of the fairway. The second has to clear more water which ends at the very edge of the green, and if the tee-shot was on the short side it pays to lay in front of the water and go for a sure bogey or, if he can produce a magical pitch and leave it dead, an ego-massaging par.

All the water is alive with fish and that most elegant of birds, the heron, is part of the habitat and very evident. There are apparently examples of royal herons about but they are not so much in evidence.

The tenth hole has water lurking to catch a sliced tee-shot but the eleventh is a straightforward par three. From the twelfth to the seventeenth you play with pine trees lining the fairways which seem to be a little more generous than those at Pals, and on the first of these you should play your tee-shot to the left side of the fairway to open up the green. The par five thirteenth favours a draw off the tee but don't overdo it or you'll find the bunkers lining the fairway at the fall of the drive. The fifteenth deserves the title of the signature hole on this course: there are two routes to the green, the surer being to the left of the water but it is longer, or you can play to the strip of fairway in between water leaving yourself a short approach to the green, which again has water right up to its edge. It is a very pretty hole viewed from any angle.

The long sixteenth with the drive over water and a difficult shot to the tightly bunkered green produces more double bogeys than would seem possible on a par five so the golfer is entitled to feel pleased with himself if he does make par. The eighteenth offers two routes from the tee, either at and, hopefully, over the vast bunker going straight in the direction of the green, or follow the fairway to the left which is longer but still leaves only a short third to the final green, once more fronted by water.

Another characteristic of a quality course apart from its intrinsic fairness as a test of golf is that you feel good after even a poor round, knowing that if you have not played well a challenging layout will always exact a high price while, perversely, leaving you anxious to play it again to prove yourself capable of standing the test, and that's how the golfer should feel after his round at Empordà Golf Club.

The clubhouse is stylishly decorated and decently restrained from the outside, in total contrast to a monstrously ugly block of flats close by, built speculatively by the sponsors of the club, one imagines, and to which the architect has managed to give the appearance of a prison block from the side you see as you enter the club from the road and something approaching the look of a Japanese multi-level driving range from the other side. This in surroundings where high design skills and a commitment to preserving the natural character of the land are memorably evident – it defies all comprehension!

Els Aiguamolls de l'Empordà

On the bay of Roses a strip of marshy land running along the edge of the coast forms the Natural Park of the *Aiguamolls*. The total area of the park is 4,783 hectares of which 850 have controlled access for the public, and this makes it the second largest wetlands in Catalonia after the area of the delta of the Ebro. As a home to numerous species of birds and a resting point for others migrating between northern Europe and the north of Africa, it is an obligatory outing for bird watchers. The Cortalet information centre organizes visits to the park which has five observatories for viewing the birds. Most people's experience is that a casual visit to the *Aiguamolls* on your own will be disappointing because from the roads that run through the park you rarely see anything more than a starling so it is advisable to put yourself in the hands of the professionals, who will make sure you do get to see some of the wildlife.

The two districts which form the area known as L'Empordà, the Alt (high) Empordà and the Baix (low) Empordà, run from the French border in the north down to a little below San Feliú de Guíxols on the Costa Brava. We are still within the province of Girona but the landscape here is very different from the densely forested land to the west of the capital of the province. The Alt Empordà which ends just below the fishing port of L'Escala is mostly flat, the occasional hill standing out from miles away, and is largely farming land with good fertile soil and enough rainfall to provide for the accumulation of water for irrigation in the summer months. As you drive around the green countryside dotted with solid masias and see the extent of the farming of the cultivatable land, and add to that the tourist business on the coast, it is not surprising to learn that Girona is the second most prosperous province in Spain after the Balearic Islands. There does not seem to be an acre of unfarmed land anywhere outside the often quite extensive woods of cork trees, raw material for the local cork industry and which are mostly found in the Baix Empordà. Apart from its famous coastline and the fact that the two best golf courses in Catalonia, L'Empordà Golf Club and Club Golf de Pals are natural attractions for those with a golfing connection, the area's excellent cuisine, numerous mediaeval villages and the appeal of visits to such places as the homes and museum of Salvador Dalí and the marvellous old buildings and streets of Girona make this area a very attractive base for part of your stay in Catalonia.

The mediaeval villages of Ullastret, Peretallada, Pals and Vulpellac

You can fill in a very pleasant afternoon just driving round and paying short visits to these halcyon villages, and if you decide to do them in one outing it makes sense to visit them either in the order given in the title to this section or in the reverse order, depending on your starting point; a glance at the map will confirm why. Nearly all the small villages in the Empordà are old – most date back at least five hundred years or more – and attractive to visit but these five enjoy almost unspoilt surroundings, for once the local authorities having had the good sense in modern times not to allow any blocks of flats or tinny industrial buildings to be built within the municipal limits or in the case of Pals, within the limits of the historical centre. Almost everywhere in Catalonia the push for modernization and industrialization in the sixties and seventies took priority over any considerations of preserving the natural beauty of these historic places and consequently some quite hideous constructions frequently spoil what would otherwise be places of considerable charm and atmosphere; there's nothing that makes you feel more of a Luddite than suddenly coming across a really splendid vista only to have it ruined by a modern industrial building, its walls covered in some obnoxious colour, taking pride of place in the foreground.

Ullastret is almost a living tableau of what a staged presentation of a Catalan mediaeval village would be: it is unreally perfect. To begin with, almost no one is out in the streets, at least in the afternoon, just an occasional pedestrian on his way somewhere. There is a complete absence of all the ugly appendages of modern life, no billboards, not even traffic lights, nothing that will detract from the old simple buildings, so weathered over the centuries that they just seem a part of nature. You can stroll round the cobbled streets running between the ancient walls of the villagers' homes in less than twenty minutes because it really is quite a small hamlet. One feature that will draw your attention is the prison! Yes, such a tiny place evidently required one, and it is, in fact, a round tower rising up in a quite central point in the village. At some stage in its history the community expanded outside the defensive walls, which today are a prominent feature you will see well inside Ullastret's cluster of buildings. The church of *Sant Pere* has a formidably imposing bell tower which has scanned the surrounding area ever since the eleventh century. At the end of your visit you will leave the place with reluctance.

Peretallada is a village with strong fortifications and these are reasonably well preserved in the central part, with three towers and a defensive trench. The centre of the village is full of narrow streets running between stone walls around the castle of Peretallada with its big central tower and squared-off parapets.

Pals is a case apart compared to the other villages mentioned because many of its buildings have been extensively restored by, one suspects, people from Barcelona with deep enough pockets to be able to create a very desirable and comfortable weekend residence. The result may be despised as 'tarted-up mediaeval', a criticism the purists level at this and other examples of perhaps overdone restorations but a wander round this agreeable old place, the centre of which is a pedestrian precinct, leaves most visitors' mouths watering with envy. Chocolate box pretty it may be, and cute rather than genuinely original, but you never see nor hear of a house up for sale!

The village of Vulpellac sounds Wagnerian but the producer of a video of the place, if anyone were to make one, would probably play a soothing piece by Purcell as background music. Like the others, in this village a placid, tranquil calm pervades and nothing visual nor audible will spoil your enjoyment of its historic buildings. Predominant in the central area the church and, adjacent to it, a large high fortress in an excellent state of repair and still in some kind of use today reward closer inspection as you walk round the streets, at one point passing through a defensive tower to gain access to another street just as people have been doing for the last five hundred years or so. Vulpellac is just another pleasing example of a rural community living a no doubt full and healthy life in surroundings which to the locals is simply home but to the visitor, feeling mentally breathless, perhaps, from the dizzy tempo of modern life, may seem more like something close to a quiet corner of paradise on earth.

Club Golf de Pals

Prior to 1990 when the Bonmont Terres Noves course, designed by Robert Trent Jones, was built near Salou on the Costa Daurada, Pals was considered to be the best test of golf in Catalonia. Many still rate it more highly than Bonmont and even than the prestigious layout at the Empordà club just down the road. Located right on the coast between Cape Bagur and the town of l'Estartit, and carved out of pine woods fringing a magnificent beach, these eighteen holes are on flat terrain which means one's physical stamina will not be severely tested.

As you approach the course heading towards the beach from the village of Pals you will know you are on the right track when you get your first glimpse of the gigantic aerial array of Radio Liberty, America's propaganda weapon aimed at Eastern Europe during the cold war. Two of the masts are as high as a twenty-storey building, and festooned between is a network of wires beaming out news and information to whoever tunes in to these stations. To the layman the array is so colossal that you are inclined to think that an astronaut on the moon with a battery operated transistor would pick it up better than anything Mission Control might beam at him. Fortunately, once you have got over the surprise of your first sight of it you scarcely notice the thing unless there is a decent wind blowing, when you play golf to a symphony of wails, whistles and moans as the wind blows through the cables.

The Club Golf de Pals, inaugurated in 1966, is this golfer's preferred model of a sensibly run golf club. The design of the clubhouse is a credit to the architect, quite simple, practical but comfortable, and singularly unobtrusive from the outside; for example, it is a safe bet that a first-time visitor to the course playing his tee-shot on the par three ninth to a green right beside the terrace adjacent to the clubhouse, would never even notice that he was, in fact, back there. He would just see the trees, the lake, the green surrounded by grass banks and perhaps be aware of a shadowy area to the left, which if you really focus on it turns out to be the clubhouse. Affairs inside the building are conducted as unobtrusively and efficiently as the building itself, and without a legion of staff; by some miracle of organization helped perhaps by the very good subsoil, the course itself is maintained in championship condition year round with a very modest number of ground staff. This compares with another club in Catalonia with over forty employees on their payroll, whose record of course maintenance has habitually been among the worst in the region, the monthly dues the highest and where you can be kept waiting forever to be served a drink in the bar if you don't personally go in pursuit of a waiter. Pals is a paragon that all Catalan clubs would do well to follow.

Wind, or to be more precise, a specific wind from the north to north-east called the Tramontana, is a conditioning factor on all the courses in the districts of the Alt Empordà and Baix Empordà. This wind affects all of the Gulf of Lyon and is the same phenomenon as the Mistral, the name the French give it from Marseilles to the Italian border although they, too, call it Tramontana in the Roussillon region. It is singularly fierce, can blow at over 130 kilometres an hour and lasts anything from one day to a week, always accompanied by clear blue skies. Driving around the coastal area on both sides of the border you will see tall windbreaks, usually cypress trees, everywhere in the countryside, essential protection from the wind for all crops. You sometimes hear Catalans from other areas say that the inhabitants of the Empordà are all slightly crazy, their brains unhinged by the wind, and it is an established fact that the cows produce less milk on the days the Tramontana blows. Crews of sailing yachts who have experienced the strength and the suddenness with which this wind can blow up as far south as Menorca and the north-eastern tip of Mallorca, usually have a dark corner in their memory, the shadow of an experience lived when, even if they were anchored in port, a frantic effort was required just to keep their boat from being battered against a quay astern. Nelson considered the worst week of bad weather in his entire career at sea was one suffered in the Mediterranean. If the Tramontana is blowing, forget golf!

This is not the course for the golfer who can hit it a mile off the tee but whose control of direction is somewhat erratic. A glance down the first fairway before wandering on to the driving range to loosen up will be enough to convince your virtuoso of the links that today he is going to have to hit it straight! Anything that wanders off the reasonably generous fairways will be in the pine trees and will require sacrificing a stroke to bail out, and there are only four holes that are not conditioned by trees on both sides of the fairway.

The view from the first tee, repeated more or less on the majority of the holes, is of a fairway uncommonly verdant against the darker green of the pine needles and the grey-brown tree trunks, with a narrow belt of short rough on either side bordering it. Depending on the angle of the sun this intense greenness is a characteristic of the course, almost too green to be true. The one consolation if the ball does end up in the woods is that there is virtually no undergrowth, just a carpet of pine needles, so you will always find it, probably startling an occasional squirrel scampering about the pines as you go to retrieve it. The second shot to the smallish greens on most of the holes requires accuracy to avoid the carefully sited bunkers, whose sand is fine and predictable.

The greens are mostly flat, some as flat as it is possible to make a green, and evenly paced so putting is not a factor which will make one's score climb at Pals.

The quality of the turf on the fairways is as good as you will find, the product of the sandy subsoil which keeps them firm and dry all through the year. If your man has been struggling with his control of direction on the first few holes the sixth hole, a friendly little par three running 151 metres (165 yards), will give him some relief provided he hits it as far as the green. Three awkward pine trees in the fairway pose a problem, not apparent from the tee, for the second shot to the green of the seventh: it pays to play the drive to the right side of the fairway. The eighth is a straightforward par five which should boost morale prior to facing an iron over the little lake to the green of the ninth, played from a tee as pretty as they come.

For the tenth and eleventh holes the trees again are the conditioning factor but the twelfth has a wide open fairway which is as well because it's long at 387 metres (423 yards) and is the stroke index 1 hole. Then he will be back in the woods again until he reaches the long, wide 492 metres (538 yards) par five sixteenth, played with Radio Liberty in your sights behind the green. The par five eighteenth is a good finishing hole with the trees encroaching on both sides of the fairway conditioning the second shot.

When he adds up his score on completing this par seventy three course with a SSS of seventy three the maestro should feel elated if he is only a couple over his handicap, which will be a good time to suggest he takes you somewhere special for dinner to celebrate, and Mas de Torrent is only minutes down the road. If the idea of a four-star hotel less than a minute from the beach and no more than five from the first tee appeals you could stay at Hotel La Costa, which also has favourable green fee rates (phone: 972-667740).

X X X

Mas de Torrent
This member of the Relais and Chateaux chain of hotels whose five-word ideal of offering 'Character, Courtesy, Charm, Calm and Cuisine' is unfailingly achieved, is ideally located both as a base for you to enjoy everything in the Empordà and for the golfer to play the courses in the

province of Girona. Of course, when he finds out what it's going to cost him, he will produce several unconvincing reasons for wanting to go somewhere else but if you catch him with the proposal on a day he's had a low score you will, as you know, find it much easier to persuade him.

The hotel is a converted masia, originally built in 1751 and lying just outside the village of Torrent, which in turn is only a few minutes from Pals, and it has managed to retain much of the character of a masia with what, for modern times, is a somewhat anarchic but very cozy layout by keeping some of the building's original floor plan. As a result there are several little sitting or reading rooms connected by small passageways, all warmly and tastefully decorated and a pleasure to relax in. Obviously some new building has had to be done, including an annex to provide additional bedrooms, but if you can, reserve one of the ten bedrooms in the main building because they are furnished with antiques and decorated in style. There is a pleasant garden, a terrace for drinks and a swimming pool, as well as a Pelota court (*frontón*), paddle tennis and bikes for the use of the guests.

Even if you decide not to stay at Mas de Torrent at least try the cuisine, which is something special in the area and makes this is an ideal venue to celebrate something, your birthday perhaps, or his best round of the week, the latter being a good custom to establish early in your holiday because it acknowledges you are entitled to similar pleasures at least once a week. The list of first courses on a recent menu included some imaginative dishes such as Carpaccio of octopus with mango and a lentil vinaigrette, and spider crab ravioli with sheep's brains and a wild mushroom sauce. There are good selections of fish and meat for the entrée and some interesting house desserts, and the wine list is up to the cuisine, if pricey. In summer you can eat out on the terrace.

Castelló d'Empúries

If you decide to follow the route through the four mediaeval villages by starting at the northern end it is worthwhile calling in at Castelló d'Empúries, a small township, before starting the drive down to Ullastret, if only to see the church of *Santa Maria*, referred to locally as 'The Cathedral' although it is no such thing. The label has its origin in the fourteenth century when Count Pere I, who governed the area, tried unsuccessfully to get the church upgraded to a cathedral. It is, however, an impressive piece of architecture, considered the second most important religious monument in the province after Girona cathedral. Building started in the mid-thirteenth century and was completed in the fourteenth and the central nave is unusual in that it enjoys quite excellent natural lighting from the large windows that run along the south wall. There is a magnificent altar-piece in carved alabaster featuring the patroness of the town, the Virgin Candelera, and the church also has an elegant eighteenth-century organ of German origin.

Outside the 'cathedral', the thirteenth-century *Pont Vell*, a Gothic arched bridge is in good repair, and the *San Domènech* convent which today houses the town hall and offices, is another building you should see.

Golf Club Peralada

If someone were to look for an area which has easy access to four high quality golf courses, each of very different character and none of them easy, the district of the Empordà fits the bill perfectly, and together with the Empordà Golf Club, the course at Pals and Club Golf d'Aro, this course at Peralada completes the quartet. It is the most northern of the four while the course at Platja d'Aro, the most southern, is only seventy kilometres away across country, and if you drive another six kilometres to Santa Cristina d'Aro you can add the course of the Club de Golf Costa Brava to the others to make it a quintet. For further variety the course at Torremirona, not described in this book, is also quite close to Figueres.

This is a venue that you, too, will enjoy because the little village of Peralada has plenty to fill your day and even your night if the annual summer music festival is on or if you enjoy a flutter at the roulette tables, while that gifted stroker of the ball foils with the thrusts and feints that the designers, Tecnoa from Barcelona, have built into the character of this course. At 5,886 metres (6,437 yards) from the yellow tees and a par of seventy two these eighteen holes, opened in 1993, pose a variety of legitimate problems on a layout which is virtually flat.

The quality of the construction, maintenance and even the small details out on the course such as the cart paths and the benches alongside the tees, are in the category of the course at Fontanals in La Cerdanya: the greens, even in mid-winter, are fast, true and unblemished; the rough is thick and wiry but not high, which penalizes the off-line shot but does not make it difficult to find the ball, and the fairways are so good that again in winter you do not need to place your ball. The clubhouse stands well in the landscape and has been kept sensibly small even if those accustomed to more baronial splendours in their own clubhouse may find the individual shower booths something of a tight fit and the supply of hot water distinctly volatile.

From the first tee the wide sweep of the plain of the Alt Empordà extends all round you, fringed to the north by the foothills of the Pyrenees and away to the north-west by the snow-capped peaks of the mountains proper. Away to the east lie the sierras that rise up behind the coast, and in the foreground the towers of Peralada castle and the village's church spire stand proud of the ancient houses, and of immediate concern to the golfer the first fairway stretches gently away to the east, only 289 metres (316 yards) to the flag and, barring one fairway bunker, a doddle of a hole. It's no gift of a par though if the wind is blowing as only the wind in this area can blow, and that is a factor which very much conditions play here as everywhere else in the Empordà.

A lot of young Umbrella Pine saplings have been planted down the rough to separate the holes, and these are supplemented by stands of small cork and olive trees at different points on the course. A nice detail for the visitor is that small signs in among the trees tell you what variety they are in Catalan and English.

The second hole opens the serious interrogation of the player by obliging him to stay on the fairway or else! If he does but his drive did not have sufficient metreage he has to decide whether to risk going for the green, fronted by a storm drain, or lay up. The fifth hole is pretty and difficult, (like some golf widows?) and has much the flavour of many of the holes at Valderrama: the tee-shot has to be placed in just the right point in the fairway otherwise there is no clear shot to the green which is dog-legged away to the left, its approach bordered on both sides by tall cork trees whose branches spread in towards the fairway. The tee of the sixth has the best view from the course out over the plain fading away in the distant haze, with Dalí's town of Figueres clearly visible and the snowed-over crests of the nearer mountains reminding the golfer that he can always take to his skis for fun if his golfing frustrations are getting the better of him. Having sopped up the view, the player can re-crank up his concentration and decide which is the best way of playing this 183 metre (200 yard) par three with another storm drain lying in wait about thirty metres in front of the green, which is further protected down the right side by a small plantation of cork trees. The eighth requires beaming a drive some 180 metres (197 yards) to the bounce to clear a lake of swans, that prospect alone being enough to induce bets all round.

The second nine are a little less demanding until you reach the stroke index 1 sixteenth, a 352 metres (385 yards) par four, with another small lake fronting almost to the green. The seventeenth, a par five, has a ditch a few metres in front of the green so again you must be well within range after your second if you are going to go for the flag with your third. If all has gone well with the round so far the eighteenth can still spoil your card with its unforgiving tee-shot: water to the right and out-of-bounds to the left, unless you are confident of clearing the water with your drive.

The course has hosted the Open de Catalunya once and several PGA qualifying schools so it is a challenge to be respected. Around the perimeter some attractive residences have been built in masia style but with modern techniques, and they all sit facing south, solid and defiant against the prevailing wind that can howl down at them from the north. The club looks set to prosper.

X X X

Peralada village

This village was not included with those previously mentioned because there is more to see here than just some mediaeval streets and houses, which do exist in abundance and are as attractive as in the other villages, and so merits at least a half-day visit.

The title of Count of Peralada existed when this area formed part of the Carolingian domain known as the Hispanic Marches in the ninth century. The title as such disappeared from 1078, when the holder, Count Ponç Hug, changed the extent of the land to be administered by his successor in his will and furthermore placed it under the Countship of Empúries, until 1599 when Philip II restored it to Viscount Francisco Jofre de Rocabertí, whose family had come into possession of the lands of the lords of Peralada in the mid-thirteenth century through marriage. The Rocabertí family, whose own title of Viscounts dates back a thousand years to the ninth century – not what you would call 'Johnny-come-latelys' – were to remain the holders of the title of Counts of

Peralada and of the palace you see today until the last Countess died without heirs in 1899.

The present-day castle is what most people imagine such a building would have looked like in its original condition, complete with crenelated battlements, a lake, and stonework in prime condition with the ivy and bougainvillea disputing the right to add the floral decoration. That it should be in this state today is to the credit of Miguel Mateu, an industrialist with, evidently, a passion for things historical who bought it in 1923. The original mansion was destroyed by a fire that razed most of the town to the ground in 1285, and the existing building was constructed half way through the fourteenth century outside the new walled town. Documents record that the two monarchs Pedro the Ceremonious and Sibiola of Fortià stayed for a few weeks at the Rocabertí palace in 1384 while waging war against the Count of Empúries, and down the centuries the palace underwent several transformations; the last such prior to Don Miguel Mateu's restorations was at the end of the nineteenth century.

Today the building is divided into two parts: one is the private residence of the family and it is not open to the public, and the other has been leased to Casinos de Catalunya and is, in fact, a casino. Even if you are not a gambler it is well worth visiting the rooms of the casino which are simply spectacular, and you can also dine in baronial splendour in the restaurant, and enjoy the gardens during the day.

Adjacent to the palace and connected to it by a bridge is the *Carmen* convent which forms part of the guided tour of the buildings open to the public. The history of the Carmelite nuns in the convent goes back to the late fourteenth century although the land had been granted to them a century earlier and they stayed there until 1837, when they were evicted under the secularization laws, an episode in one of Spain's periodic outbursts against the Church, its accumulated wealth, its always over-cozy association with the conservative Establishment, and its perceived privileged status; the convent church was turned into a theatre and the adjacent buildings into housing for the townspeople. In an astonishing example of a contractual right being recognized almost six hundred years after the contract was written, the last of the Peralada Countesses, Juana, recovered the buildings in 1855 by virtue of a reversion clause established when the land had originally been ceded by Count Dalmau de Rocabertí to the Carmelites in 1293!

Such was the collection of buildings which Miguel Mateu purchased in 1923 and which he was to restore extensively as well as adding a voluminous collection of historical miscellanea embracing the period from the Greek colonization of Empúries to the nineteenth century, and substantially increasing the library, which originated in the time of the Counts, all of which you can see.

The library today has over 72,000 books, making it the largest private library in Catalonia, and while the reading room is a bibliophile's dream, for the casual visitor it is also a singular experience. Among the many noteworthy volumes are more than a thousand different editions of *El Quijote* embracing thirty three languages, including Japanese, Persian, Indonesian and Hebrew, and a first edition of part one printed in 1605 by Ulma in Germany and illustrated by hand. There is the book of *Pandectas y Decretales*, a code of Roman law, from the fourteenth century and Ptolomeo's map of 1482 as well as personally dedicated books from Dalí and Josep Pla to Don Miguel, whose daughter and the present owner, Carmen, continues to add to this extraordinary collection of books and documents.

The convent cloister is late fourteenth-century Gothic, beautifully restored and embellished with some of the items from the historical collection including tombs, tablets, sculptures and capitals from different periods. It was probably completed at the same time as the church, around 1400.

The convent church, which is the family's private chapel, consists of a nave with a richly-coloured, carved ceiling, and the patterned floor is the motif of the Rocabertí coat-of-arms. Its recent restoration gives it a modern sheen which somehow does not quite fit with its true age but that is how it must have looked when it was first completed. The chapel can be hired for weddings as indeed can the library if a civil wedding is preferred, provided that the reception is held in the the private rooms of the casino. A curious detail in the carved capital on one of the pillarets supporting the altar is the basis for historians dating it at 1285: the capital has the three escutcheons of the Counts of Barcelona, Empúries and Rocabertí, and as all three of them together with their respective militia spent most of the time hacking and chopping away at each other to try and gain territory, the only time they joined forces to fight a common enemy was when the French invaded the area in that year.

The Mateu historical collection, apart from those items in the cloister and church, is on display in the museum housed in a large hall forming the west wing of the cloister. It includes Graeco-Roman glassware, Punic and Egyptian items either from Empúries itself or from other points on the Mediterranean coast, pottery, ceramics and crystal from France, Germany, Italy and other areas of Spain and Catalonia, and some good collections of coins from the Greeks down to nineteenth-century Spain.

Coin collections do not usually arouse much excitement in the non-collector but sometimes they can provoke some stimulating associations and contrasts of ideas. Here are three items which most people would find lodge for a while in their memories: first, Roman silver coins which were the legal tender in the empire at the time of the death of Christ; for thirty of these Judas betrayed him. Secondly, coins from the Iberos, the inhabitants of the Peninsula prior to the arrival of the Romans and until comparatively recently considered to be little better than primitive barbarians, which are further proof of the relative sophistication of their society whose cultural legacy reveals a surprising degree of aesthetic achievement and which is now the subject of extensive study; the culture of the Iberos was recently given monographic exhibitions in Paris and in Spain. Thirdly, the first peseta to be introduced as a new currency in Spain which occurred in Catalonia in 1808 during the Napoleonic occupation; the central government did not start coining pesetas until sixty years later.

The peseta was to be a truly decimalized currency: the one centimo coin was made of copper and weighed one gram while the peseta coin was made of silver and weighed five grams, so a hundred two-peseta coins, each weighing ten grams, amounted to a kilo of silver! Today, two hundred pesetas would buy you about seven grams of silver. A case has been made, in Catalonia of course, to explain the choice of the word 'peseta': it is said to derive from the Catalan word '*peça*', meaning a piece, the diminutive of which is '*peceta*', pronounced exactly the same as peseta and meaning a small piece – of silver, one supposes.

The final stage of the tour of the palace and convent buildings takes you to the wine museum and winery where Castillo de Peralada Cava and table wines are produced. In the wine museum you can see 300-year-old vats made of oak and rectangular in shape. To enable them to be rolled along the floor there are big wooden rings made up of sections of olive tree branches, which being naturally curved on the tree can be

joined together to make a circle forming a wooden wheel round each
end of the vats. Olive wood is one of the hardest there is, so hard in fact
that it doesn't float.

If your trip to Catalonia takes place towards the end of July or in
August you will probably coincide with the annual summer Castell de
Peralada International Music Festival, which usually lasts about three
weeks. A covered stage and orchestra pit are erected in the gardens and
the spectators are seated on scaffolding forming an auditorium under
the summer night sky. It has now established a solid reputation after
eleven editions, and since the beginning has offered a wide choice of
music ranging from opera to pop singers but with the emphasis mainly
on classical music. The setting at night from a seat perched high up on
the banked scaffolding is an experience to remember: behind the stage
the illuminated mediaeval walls and buildings of the village form a
natural and very theatrical backdrop, and above you the contrasting
blackness of the sky, with just the occasional star visible through the
glow from the stage unless you are fortunate enough to coincide with a
moonlit night, forms a vast cosmic dome above you. You can of course
be unlucky and begin to see distant flashes of lightning appear and
gradually approach as a summer storm moves in, which if it turns into
rain will bring your evening's fare of music to a watery end. The
management usually invite you to take shelter temporarily in the casino
to see if the storm passes quickly in which case the performance will be
continued. If it doesn't, you face an evening of Blackjack or Roulette.

Mas Molí

Three kilometres down the road from Peralada to Villabertran you have
the opportunity to vary your diet of Catalan cooking and enjoy a first
class roast at Mas Molí, an old mill house tastefully converted into a
restaurant right beside the road, where the cut of meat is roasted in an
old-fashioned, wood-fired baking oven with the glowing embers inside
the oven itself, as in Castilla. Tender roast lamb and suckling pig are the
specialities of the house, and unless you are averse to pork the latter,
called *cochinillo* in Spanish, can be unreservedly recommended, the
crackling crisp and the meat so tender that the ritual, common in
Castillian restaurants, of separating the *cochinillo* into portions using a
kitchen plate as a knife is performed at your table. A two-year-old
Castillo de Peralada tinto crianza (matured in the cask) goes well with

the roast, and a little *Manchego* cheese followed by a glass of *semi sec cava* will round off the meal in style.

Sant Pere de Rodes

The founder of this imposing monastery must have been a firm believer in the principle that the higher up and nearer to the heavens you site a religious house the closer the inmates will feel to the Almighty. Towering above the bay of Port de la Selva, what remains of this vast Romanesque group of buildings will uplift your spirits too, if only because of the view. To get there, though, you first have to undergo the purgatory of a tortuous road that claws its way up the 600-metre-high Sierra de Roses from Vilajuiga, a village just off the N-260 running between Figueres and Port Bou. Once there, you can enjoy these impressive buildings which include the splendid bell tower of the church, the remains of the cloister, the monks' living quarters, the abbot's palace, and the cellar – you may have guessed, correctly, that this monastery belonged to the Benedictines, a religious order that sensibly tempers austerity with one or two of the comforts of life. To see it at its most impressive you need to have arrived there just as the east-facing walls redden in the glow of the early morning sun.

The last monks to inhabit the monastery left in 1731, tired of the constant attacks of marauding smugglers and pirates. Although there are records of the community as far back as the ninth century what you see today dates from the twelfth. By 1215 there were twenty five monks in residence and it was in the thirteenth and fourteenth centuries that the community was at its most prosperous, and the monastery was fortified and became a defensive base against piracy. In spite of this it was constantly attacked and plundered in the seventeenth century, and in 1693 the Duc de Noailles, in the course of a war between Spain and France, seized the famous Bible of Rodes and took it back to France; it can be seen today at the Bibliothèque Nationale de Paris.

Empúries

Just outside the small fishing port of l'Escala on the gulf of Roses are the remains of the only ancient Greek settlement to the west of Italy whose layout is known today. Founded in the sixth century BC this Neàpolis, or new city, was known as Emporeion and was built on what was then a small island just off the coast but today is on the mainland right beside the beach. It had over three hundred houses and a population of around 2,500 inhabitants. Close to it and only a few hundred metres inland the Romans built a town of their own between the second and first centuries BC, apparently to attack Hannibal's lines of communication from Carthage to Italy, which he had already reached. It developed into an important city in Rome's control of the Iberian Peninsula but later lost influence due to the rise of Tarraco (Tarragona) as the main Roman centre in the north, and finally disappeared as a town when the Visigoths invaded the peninsula in the third century AD.

You can visit the remains of both towns and see items of archaeological interest from the Greeks, Romans and even the Iberian tribes who inhabited the area before the Greeks arrived in the Monographical Museum of Empúries, which stands within the precinct of the ruins.

It would be a shame to miss the opportunity of eating a dish of anchovies from l'Escala – *anchoves de l'Escala* – while you are here. Technically, an anchovy is a variety of small sardine (*Sardinella allecia*), commonly called a *boquerón* in Spanish, which has been immersed in salt, oil and herbs for forty days prior to canning. The local fishing fleet catches them in large amounts and they are processed in the town. You can eat them as they are, straight out of the tin, or on *pan con tomate*, which is how most people prefer them. For something more substantial you could try a *suquet de peix*, a fish stew, very much a favourite anywhere on the Catalan coast but particularly so on the Costa Brava. A mixture of different types of fish are steamed while some cloves of garlic, strips of green pepper and a purée of fresh, peeled tomatoes are sautéed. Once browned, finely sliced potatoes and the fish plus its broth are added to the sautéed items and left until everything is cooked, when diced garlic, parsley and almond are added just prior to serving. It tastes as good as it sounds.

Club de Golf Costa Brava

Just a few kilometres inland from San Felíu de Guíxols lies the village of Santa Cristina de Aro and bordering on it, on rising wooded ground, the residential development and golf course of the Club de Golf Costa Brava. Opened in 1968 this is considered for various reasons in Catalan golfing circles one of the classic courses, not so much for the quality of design of the course itself but more because it is relatively accessible from

Barcelona and Perpignan, making it an attractive place for a weekend home. Also the character of the layout is quite different from those of Pals and Empordà, and only the golfer who is really on his game will play to his handicap which, as you are only too aware, equates to him being at his best afterwards, full of smiles and good humour, considerate, and possibly even generous as well. Just like he was when you first met him!

It would be a mistake for you not to drop in and walk round the very pleasant clubhouse, a beautiful old masia perfectly adapted inside to fulfil all the functions required for the members' needs and comfort, and decorated appropriately to match the character of the building. It stands well in its surroundings, a genuine handsome stone-built country house. There is a strong contingent of members from other European countries who have homes in the residential area either because they are retirees or because they use them as holiday homes. Quite a number of them are retired Dutch, many of whom, it seems, find the distance by road from Holland, something under 1,500 kilometres, a manageable enough trip by road to more or less commute every few months or so between their home in Holland and their house on the Costa Brava. For the English-speaking golf visitor it is, therefore, easy to find a game with a local member he can converse with.

The course measures 5,444 metres (5,954 yards) for a par of seventy from the yellow tees, and the first nine are quite different in character from the back half. The first two holes convince most people playing their first round here that the designer, Hamilton Stutt, must belong to the spit-in-your-eye school of golf architects, a term explained in the course that most deserves the title, Costa Daurada; the number of trees left standing in these fairways make these two holes more of an obstacle course than honest holes of golf. The first hole has a large evergreen oak standing plum in the middle of the fairway at about the 180 metre mark, just where it should not be and, of course, ensures you hit a perfectly straight drive dead centre! But this is nothing compared to what awaits the player on the second hole, where several tall pines impede a normal tee-shot completely, and if these are somehow negotiated, another tall umbrella pine virtually blankets out the entire green for the approach shot. The golfer's nervous state, if not the foul mood he will be in by now after tangling with all of this, can begin to revert to normal because hereafter if the odd tree on a few holes is positioned in the fairway there is always a route round it. The sixth, rated stroke index 1, measures 426 metres (468 yards) from the yellow tee, making it the longest par four in Catalonia.

The holes on the first nine are enjoyably varied and have been cut out of woodland but the fairways are generously wide and the greens medium sized and evenly paced. The second nine, after the first two holes, are more repetitive but mostly free of unwanted obstacles, the sixteenth making a testing par four and the eighteenth another demanding, long (372 metres, 407 yards), uphill par four to a sharply sloping green.

This is a course with plenty of character, full of handsome views away over the surrounding woods of pine and cork trees, and so a pleasure to play. It is not intrinsically difficult but it never fails to surprise most of the average handicap golfers who play it that they rarely play to their par here. If your golfer manages to do so, make the most of the opportunity. You might even persuade him to check into La Gavina, a member of Relais & Chateaux which overlooks the elegant bay of S'Agaró, for a night or two or at least have dinner there. If you prefer a little restaurant with more of a rustic atmosphere Les Panolles is only two minutes down the road and it is always a pleasure to eat in this cleverly adapted masia. As a first course you could try the *amanida de bolets amb confit de pollastre i daus de formatge fresc* (salad of wild mushrooms with chicken purée and small cheese 'dice') and for the entrée a dish from the Empordà, perhaps *bacallà amb cigrons, orella i morro de porc* (salt cod cooked with chickpeas, pig's ear and nose), or *mandonguilles amb gambetes* (meat balls with prawns). This restaurant also has a good selection of game dishes during the hunting season, which lasts from October to February, and a good cellar.

$$X \ X \ X$$

Salvador Dalí

The name of Salvador Dalí is intimately linked to the district of the Empordà, and the Dalí Triangle, as it is called and which consists of the Dalí museum in Figueres, his home in Port Lligat and the castle of Púbol where he spent a few of his last years, provides an appealing opportunity to learn more about this thoroughly exaggerated character who virtually made a career of displaying his eccentricities in public,

Salvador Dalí. Arxiu històric, Ajuntament de Barcelona.

and who lived from 1904 to 1989. In some years the Dalí museum has been the second most visited museum in Spain, preceded only by the Prado in Madrid, which gives an idea of the universal appeal his art enjoys. Some biographical background should make your visits to the Dalínian world more interesting.

Dalí was born in Figueres, the son of the town's notary and he was therefore from a conventional middle-class family. From his earliest years his behaviour and reactions to almost any event in his daily life were anything but conventional, however, revealing a vastly eccentric personality, and although his basic education with the religious order of the *Maristas* in Figueres proceeded along the established parameters of the *bachillerato*, Dalí was by no means a dedicated student. By the age of seven his exceptional artistic talent was already evident and he was receiving drawing classes from a drawing teacher, Sr. Nuñez, and it was at this age that he solemnly announced that he wanted to be Napoleon. He also spent some time with the Pichot family, friends of Dalí's father, and here Dalí was first exposed to life in the house of an artistic family: Ramón Pichot, the father, was an impressionist painter of some repute whose work enthused the young Dalí, two of the sons were musicians, one daughter was an opera singer and the other one was married to a poet. In this ambience he gave free rein to his own febrile imagination and began experimenting with different painting techniques, particularly with the effects of light in a composition.

His schooling continued under the *Maristas* although it was plainly evident that his was not to be an academic future, and it was in those years that Cadaqués, a village on the coast some thirty kilometres from Figueres, became an intimate part of Dalí's world. It was where the family spent their summers and it would become a fundamental in his painting thereafter, the jagged, rocky coastline forming the background in many of his works. After a favourable reception to an exhibition of his work in the Figueres municipal theatre, which would later become the Dalí Museum, his father put him down for the School of Fine Arts in Madrid which he entered at the age of seventeen and where he studied for five years. It was here that he met and developed close friendships with Federico Garcia Lorca, the poet, and with Luis Buñuel with whom he would later collaborate in the making of one of Buñuel's most surrealist of films, *Un Chien Andalou*. His years in art school were far from uneventful in spite of his laudable dedication night and day to painting subjects that interested him rather than his teachers, and which were much admired by his fellow students: he was punished with a year's forced absence for protesting at the appointment of a professor whom the students considered to be technically ill-prepared for the post, and later he was finally expelled for refusing to answer questions from an examining tribunal because he considered the members to be incompetent. This theatrically rebellious nature was to be the trademark of his character throughout his life.

In the summer of 1925 while he was still a student, Dalí had his first one-man exhibition at the Dalmau Gallery in Barcelona where his painting *A Girl Standing at a Window* was seen and admired by Picasso and Miró. His sister, Ana Maria, was his model for this and other paintings in those years before Dalí met his future wife, Gala, who eventually took over Ana Maria's role as model and mother figure for the impractical and sexually obsessed artist; as could be expected an undying enmity between the two women quickly developed.

In 1927 he went to Paris and visited Picasso, and a year later he joined up with the Surrealists and for the first time met the poet Paul Eluard, who was prominent in the movement, and his wife, Gala Diakonova, who had been born in Russia.

Surrealism in painting was, according to its practitioners, a concept that the idea in a painting is more important than the form used to express it, and the ideas could be anything from images seen in dreams to attempts to express thoughts from the subconscious mind. Dalí elaborated further on this with what he called his 'paranoiac-critical method'. As Nathaniel Harris in his book *The Life and Works of Dalí* aptly puts it, 'Dalí's verbal descriptions of his "paranoiac-critical method" leave most readers little wiser; but the personal effectiveness of the "method" can hardly be questioned, since it enabled Dalí to tap his unconscious and produce chains of potent, startling images.'

His 'method' invites you to think like a madman and learn to use the creative way of thinking of a madman while remaining rational. In this way, he claimed, reason and madness are combined and your imagination benefits from the obscure forces of the subconscious mind. Dalí said on more than one occasion, 'The only difference between Salvador Dalí and a madman is that I'm not mad.' Many people, startled by his extravagant behaviour when playing up to the media, must have questioned that assertion.

By 1929 Dalí, back in Spain and completely enamoured of Gala, had become psychically unbalanced and some feared for his sanity. Only Gala, when she visited him in Cadaqués in the summer with her husband and others from the Surrealist group in Paris, could calm him down and from then on she never left him. In November of the same year he had his first individual exhibition in Paris at the Galerie Goemans in which his painting, *The Lugubrious Game,* was the centrepiece. The following year he bought a fisherman's house in Port Lligat which he would transform over the years into the present, labyrinthine building where he painted so many of his works, and which became his and Gala's home.

Over the next few years he visited Paris frequently, giving numerous conferences which usually ended in rowdy chaos, and was increasingly in conflict with the Surrealists who finally excluded him from their group in 1934. The same year he travelled to the United States for the first time to find a country ideally suited to his theatrics in public. Between exhibitions of his work there were conferences, parties, masked fancy-dress balls, and all this was widely reported in the sensational press. His flamboyant exhibitionism was such that the press asked themselves if he really was a madman or just a very good businessman, the consummate self-promoter. His contemporary Surrealists were quick to condemn this commercial side of Dalí: André Breton, the arch-priest of the movement, labelled him 'Avida Dollars', an anagram of Salvador Dalí.

In 1936, the year of the outbreak of the Spanish Civil War, Dalí returned to New York where all his paintings in an exhibition there were sold on the first day. In December of the same year he appeared on the cover of *Time* magazine, confirmation of his acceptance by the American public as a figure of wide artistic acclaim. In 1940, following the onset of the Second World War, he and Gala returned to America where they were to spend the next eight years. Dalí worked tirelessly on lithographs, paintings, book illustrations and designs for the theatre and ballet. He reached the pinnacle of fame and success in these years in the United States where opportunities abounded for him to indulge all his abilities, including fashion and jewellery design, the writing of his only novel, *Hidden Faces,* design of the film-set for Alfred Hitchcock's *Spellbound,* all this while featuring as the star of many TV commercials.

As early as 1941 Dalí had announced his intention to become 'classic'. In part this may have derived from his earlier study of Italian

Renaissance artists as well as his admiration for Velázquez and Zurbarán although his paintings still reflected his brand of Surrealism. A gradual change in many of his attitudes to life and current events was taking place, however. From the tempestuous, iconoclastic – in the anti-establishment sense – rebellious young man of the twenties and thirties Dalí became deeply interested in religion, even became pro-Franco and later a convinced monarchist, and many of his later paintings were religious in theme and classical in execution. No one has ever questioned his ability as a draughtsman, some of his paintings being immensely complex, and he differed radically from other Surrealists in using a painstakingly accurate depiction of all the objects in a composition.

In 1948 he and Gala returned to Port Lligat and in 1949 he was even received by Pope Pius XII, who later blessed his painting of The Madonna of Port Lligat featuring Gala as the Madonna; Gala's rumoured sexual appetite where young men were concerned made her a questionable model for the subject. In the 1950s he continued with religious and even patriotic themes, and his annual routine was split between Paris, New York and Port Lligat, working when at home, giving heady, weird public appearances in the two capital cities and mixing with the famous of the time. While new and fast succeeding trends were the rule in the art world his painting leaned to style, order in the hierarchical sense, and tradition. In 1956 he published his book *Les Cocus du vieil art moderne*, a tract against most of the new trends in art. In fact Dalí could not stand abstract art, commenting after visiting one such exhibition that the best thing on view was the entrance door which at least had been painted with a nice smooth homogeneous coat of paint, and on another occasion he observed that abstract painters did not believe in anything, and if you don't believe in anything you won't paint anything, or hardly anything. In 1955 he gave a conference at the Sorbonne on the phenomenalistic aspects of the 'paranoiac-critical method'; he arrived in a Rolls Royce full of cauliflowers and the conference later ended in a highly publicized uproar. It was, as always, great for business.

He was married to Gala in a religious ceremony in 1958, and she eventually died in 1982 at the age of eighty eight. Dalí's retrospective exhibition at the Centre Pompidou in 1979 broke all records for attendance but by now his output of new works had declined severely, and after the death of Gala he retired to live in his castle of Púbol with his health much deteriorated. In 1986 after suffering burns in the accidental fire in Púbol castle he was taken to Figueres where he lived as a recluse, rarely leaving his room in the building adjacent to the Museum, which Dalí had renamed the *Torre Galatea*, until his death in 1989 at the age of eighty-four. He is buried in a tomb under the geodesic dome of the Museum.

Dalí's house at Port Lligat

One of the most painted views in Catalonia must be the town of Cadaqués and particularly its church and surrounding buildings as seen from the sea. Nature has conspired to give the town an air of privacy deriving from its location below steeply rising hills which virtually encircle the town, effectively closing it off from the Cape of Creus to the north and the huge bay of Roses to the south. The all-white buildings clustering up to the church built on higher ground, backed by the tree-less hills behind, the little bay in front of the town flanked by slate-grey rocks, is a temptation few artists, Dalí included, have been able to resist. Mercifully even the authorities in Franco's time when tourism was encouraged to grow at such a pace that many stretches of the Spanish Mediterranean coastline became a uniquely ugly concrete jungle, exercised enough restraint in deciding what was allowed to be built in Cadaqués to preserve its original appearance; today the town might have spread somewhat but it still looks much as it did in the thirties.

To get there requires following the somewhat serpentine road that climbs over the hills separating the town from Roses but this does not seem to discourage the tourist determined to see Cadaqués for himself because there are always plenty of them about, eating in the shade outside the numerous waterfront restaurants or visiting the Centre d'Art Perrot-Moore, a permanent private exhibition of paintings by Dalí and Picasso, or another exhibition of Dalí engravings at the Esplai Dalí. A visit to Cadaqués makes for a very complete day's excursion – memorable views over the coast as you climb up over the hills, an interesting small town to stroll round and perhaps a visit to the sixteenth-century church or just a walk out towards the sea along one side of the narrow bay to enjoy the much-painted view of the town, a visit to the art exhibitions, and finally, if you have booked ahead and reserved a visiting time, which is advisable, feasting your eyes and letting your imagination conjure up scenes of Dalí at work and relaxing as you wander through his highly unusual house at Port Lligat.

The house, a jumble of oddly shaped buildings that started with a simple fisherman's shack which Dalí bought in 1930 and to which were added others acquired over the years, is right on the water's edge of this small bay just round a promontory from Cadaqués and no more than a kilometre or so from there. Like Cadaqués it seems to be completely isolated, a tiny fishing port standing in protected water making it an unspoilt haven tucked inside the fiercely rocky coastline, and the house makes the most of the view, its windows carefully sited to give glimpses out over the water from all corners.

Inside, the house is a maze of mostly very small, oddly shaped rooms interconnected by little stairways and passages, partly open-plan in layout and giving you more sense of space and perspective than is really there. Dalí loathed modern architecture, particularly Le Corbusier's and anything deriving from it, and his house sets out to defy all tenets of conventional functional planning in the use of space; the result is very original and successful, a dwelling you would be delighted to call your own.

There is a minuscule reception room with a tiny fireplace and furniture in proportion, which must have been as cozy as anywhere in Europe in winter. The entrance hall, also small, has a large stuffed bear presiding over it. The one room that has all the space and more for its function is the bedroom which is accessed through, and open to, a kind of antechamber on a slightly lower level. Two partly canopied beds with forged iron bed-heads and bright blue bedspreads are the largest pieces of furniture in the room but the other furnishings and decorative odds and ends all add to its character, and there is the view out over the bay as the crowning glory. The adjacent bathroom is quite conventional, no doubt due to Gala's influence. The library is, within the context of this unconventional house, almost demure; Dalí's books have been taken to the Centre for Dalinian Studies in Figueres so the shelves carry simulated volumes to maintain the original effect.

The Oval Room is possibly the most unusual room in the house being circular in shape and with the walls rising up as in a dome. The effect is rather like being inside an egg in which a flat floor has been laid at its widest point. A low circular sofa runs round the wall, and this was the room used by Gala to receive friends and visitors.

Dalí's studio looks out over the water and those responsible for arranging the details inside the house now that it is on view to the public have contrived to make this room appear as if he could have been painting there yesterday.

The garden is as unconventional as the house itself with a long narrow swimming pool surrounded by bizarre objects ranging from enormous snakes to a Michelin man and a telephone booth. There is also, as you would no doubt by now have expected, a sort of throne area from which Dalí and Gala could preside over gatherings of friends and visitors who could be anything from government ministers to hippies, all mixing together and enjoying the extravagant antics of their host.

The number of visitors allowed inside the house at any one time is strictly limited because of the size of some of the rooms so it is best to reserve a time for your visit by telephone on (972) 258063. The house is currently open to the public from March to October.

Púbol Castle

Dalí bought Púbol castle, located in the village of the same name and adjacent to the larger village of La Pera (both roughly halfway between Girona and La Bisbal d'Empordà) in 1970 to fulfil his promise, made in the thirties to Gala, to give her a palace as a present. He wanted it to be her refuge to which he would only come if she invited him.

The history of Púbol castle dates back to the eleventh century, and the first owner seems to have been Gaufred de Bastons, the founder of the lineage of the Barons of Púbol. The existing castle dates from the fourteenth century and initially it had its own oratory adjacent to the castle, which later became the village church and forms an integral part of the main building. At present the church is only open on the annual Festa Major, 15 August, and on a few other special days. In the second half of the fourteenth century the castle belonged to the Gispert de Campllong family and their escutcheon, featuring a raven, appears in several places within the confines of the castle. Such was the power of the lords of the castle in those days that they could condemn people under their jurisdiction to death. The castle continued to pass from one family to another down the centuries, and when Dalí bought it for an officially recorded price of one and a half million pesetas – the real price would probably have been two or three times that – the place was a semi-ruin, uninhabited since the 1930s.

Dalí, of course, took an active role in the restoration of the building and both he and Gala wanted it to retain its aged but romantic atmosphere. The result is, for a Dalían production, almost subdued. He did a few murals on walls and ceilings, painted a false door, two false radiators and the figure of Gala on a sheet of metal, and various other small paintings, all of which are hung on the castle's walls. The garden features several figures of elephants on long legs, and the swimming pool several heads of Wagner made in mosaics. He also designed two curved fireplaces and had a 'G' for Gala placed over several doorways, an affirmation of her ownership of the building.

In keeping with Dalí's taste for theatrical effect there is a throne room with the ceiling painted by him which was intended to be the room where visitors would be received into the regal presence. In general the furnishings in the castle are strongly coloured but the furniture is all either antiques or of a fairly simple design. Contrasting with the throne room is the nice simple breakfast room. In what was part of the attic some of Gala's party dresses are on display, some of them designed by Dalí himself, and surprisingly reflect a restrained conservative taste in fashion.

Gala came and stayed in the castle regularly for a decade but rarely invited Dalí to join her although they spoke almost daily by phone. She eventually died in Port Lligat and Dalí had her body, wrapped in a blanket, brought to Púbol in his Cadillac; the car can be still seen today at the castle and the story goes that this was its last journey. Gala is buried in the vast basement crypt, her tomb guarded by the figures of a giraffe and two horses' heads.

After her death, Dalí took up residence in the castle living as a semi-recluse and seeing only those whose visit he had previously authorized. He had some of his paintings brought here from Paris and New York, and he continued painting, using the dining room as his studio until 1983, when ill-health obliged him to stop. He lived here for a period of two years which ended in the summer of 1984 when he suffered burns from a fire which broke out in his bedroom while he was asleep. After hospitalization he chose to spend what were to be the last four years of his life in the *Torre Galatea* alongside his museum in Figueres. He had designed the decoration of the building's external walls, featuring rows of loaves of bread and huge eggs which stand on-end on the cornices of the building, while living in Púbol castle.

Visits to Púbol castle can be made from mid-March to the end of September, visiting hours currently being 10.30 a.m. to 5.30 p.m. except for Mondays when it remains closed. In July, August and September it is open every day of the week from 10.30 a.m. to 7.30 p.m. but you are advised to check these details with the Gala-Dalí Foundation before making your visit.

The Dalí museum at Figueres

Dalí left his entire estate to the Spanish State which in turn has placed the organization and exhibition of his works and homes under the control of the Gala-Dalí Foundation based in the Dalí museum itself. This building in the centre of Figueres was originally the Municipal Theatre, largely destroyed in the Civil War. It was Dalí's own decision to create the museum of his work in this location: 'Where, if not in my home town, should the most extravagant and solid part of my work remain, where if not here? The Municipal Theatre, or what was left of it, seemed totally adequate to me for three reasons: first, because I am an eminently theatrical painter; secondly, because the theatre is just in front of the church where I was baptized; and thirdly, because it was precisely in the foyer of the theatre that my first exhibition was held.'

The museum is claimed to be the largest Surrealist object in the world and the influence of Dalí, who designed most of it, is evident in every detail. From the spectacular montage of a Cadillac under the geodesic dome to the examples of *trompe-l'oeil*, everything is displayed in a way designed to continually provoke the viewer's interest and challenge his powers of interpretation. There are examples of most of the artistic phases of Dalí's career on view from his early experiments with Impressionism and Cubism, and then later on his own form of Surrealism, and finally paintings from the last years of his life, all reflected in paintings, drawings, etchings, sculptures, jewellery and some highly original montages.

One room displays works from Dalí's private collection, including works by El Greco, Fortuny, Urgell, Meissonnier, Duchamp and Bouguereau.

Few people fail to be provoked or in some way visually stimulated by Dalí's unusual interpretation of the themes he chose to paint but because the thinking that lies behind each work is, to say the least, convoluted it pays to view his work with the aid of an illustrated book written by a professional art critic; if you do, your enjoyment of his work will be much increased.

Club Golf d'Aro

As you follow the road up through the residential area called Mas Nou that lies just behind Platja d'Aro on your way to this golf course the climb is so steep that you know there must be some eye-stunning views once you reach the plateau that straddles this ridge of hills, around four hundred metres high and running back inland to the west, and indeed the views from the course are the feature that everyone associates with Club Golf d'Aro. If the weather is fine you can happily leave the golfer to hack his way round eighteen holes while you enjoy a morning's ramble and take in the sensational views over the coast and surrounding countryside. It would be difficult to match these splendid vistas anywhere else in Catalonia outside the Pyrenees.

For the golfer the views are a distraction he could do without because this fine course, designed by Ramón Espinosa, is a very stern test of golf, and he will need some unwavering concentration to do himself justice. He will also have to hit the ball very straight because wayward direction on most of the holes means disaster, and the course is long, too, at 6,004 metres (6,566 yards) from the yellow tees.

Everything about this layout has a touch of quality to it and requires golf of high quality as well for a decent result. The fairways are always in prime condition, the generous greens are consistently paced and not overly difficult to read, and because this is a very heavily bunkered course only a properly executed shot to the green has any hope of avoiding sand. Most of the holes pose a problem from the tee that is unique to that hole, and the par fives can set you a testing second shot as well. Because many of the fairways border on ravines and often slope in the direction of danger it can be imperative to place the tee-shot in exactly the right area of the fairway to keep the ball in play so the player who is good with a long iron off the tee will be at something of an advantage. Few courses manage to achieve so much variety of character from one hole to another, and this one is a credit to its designer in this and every other respect.

The first two holes do not give the player much indication of what is to follow unless he pulls his tee-shot badly to the left on the first, which would mean a lost ball. By the fourth hole, a par five, the dangers of playing on the edge of steep ravines are plain to see, and if his second strays left it will be a case of '*Adiós, Bonita!*'. On the sixth, the handicap-one rated hole, he must place his tee-shot close to the left hand border of the fairway because beyond the line of vision from the tee the ground slopes steeply to the right. The ninth could almost be called the signature hole on this course because it exemplifies the tightness to be handled on most of the layout; it must be one of the narrowest par fours in Catalonia, with a 200-metre-deep ravine to the left and a road in front of a wood to the right. In some places the fairway is barely twenty metres wide. The tenth, a little wider, still needs a laser-straight tee-shot to avoid ravines both left and right. And so on!

If you decide to accompany the golfer for at least part of his round you will find some notable viewing spots out over the surrounding area. From the first fairway you already see way out to the north across densely wooded terrain, and from the fourth tee across to the sierra running to the south of Santa Cristina de Aro some twelve kilometres away. From the fifth tee you have a bird's-eye view over S'Agaró bay and part of San Feliú de Guíxols, and if you decide to stick with him to the bitter end – of this round, that is – there is a great view from the fifteenth north-east to Palamos about fourteen kilometres away over the woods.

Because you are on land four hundred metres up from sea level the wind can be strong and, in winter, distinctly fresh. Low cloud lying on the course can be another problem between December and April so you must pick your day on the day for visiting this club in the winter months. Recently, the club has installed an electrified cattle fence round the perimeter of the course to keep out the wild boars (*senglars* in Catalan and *jabalí* in Spanish), which inhabit the surrounding woods and which tear up fairways and rough although never the greens with their tusks looking for grubs. They can cause havoc in a night and there are few courses in the region that do not suffer from this problem. They never invade a course during the day, apparently, but if you were confronted with one either shin smartly up the nearest tree or take to your heels because they are notoriously aggressive!

It might be a good idea to have a little surprise ready for him after the round, like a new box of golf balls, because if he's had a difficult day his mood could be other than the holiday kind, and he's sure to have lost a few balls. Depending on how deep is his gloom you could also invite him out for a really good meal in the evening at Eldorado Petit on the Rambla in San Feliú de Guíxols, where a little *mousse de erizos de mar* (sea urchins) makes an appetizing starter. If it happens to be Wednesday or November, when it closes, try Can Toni on Calle Santa Martirià, which will cost you less but where you will also eat very well.

III

Barcelona

Real Club de Golf 'El Prat'

As you skirt round Barcelona airport on the perimeter road on your way
to this golf club one feature of the course is already apparent: it is dead
flat, built on the delta of the Llobregat river. As you arrive at the club
other first impressions accumulate fast: the tidy row of tangerine trees,
loaded with fruit, lining the last part of the access road into the club; the
guard on duty at the entrance wearing, until recently, what appeared to
be gamekeeper's livery, and then the group of chauffeurs chatting
together as you park under the pine trees. Well, clearly, this is a club
where the gentleman golfer can expect to be treated with the attention
and deference he deserves. 'Like Hell he does!' as your mother would
say. Then, as you get out of your car, the first howling roar of a Boeing
shatters your illusions and maybe your eardrums, and the other feature
of the course is evident: you are right at the end of one of the airport
runways. If the runway is in use, a plane takes off roughly every four
minutes and, with its engines under full load and whining, climbs not
very far above you as it heads out over the Mediterranean.

Most golfers can turn really quite nasty if you so much as breathe
audibly when they are somewhere in the process of executing a golf
shot, hurling a sharp comment on the virtues of silence at you once
they have completed it. The members at El Prat are a different breed.
You could have a supersonic flying display by Concorde going on
directly above them without them noticing anything and, indeed, they
probably feel lonesome and abandoned by the world on any other golf
course. One has to admit that, with the exception of the seventeenth tee
on the Yellow course, which is only about eighty metres from the end
of the runway and you always wonder if the jet accelerating towards
you is going to reach take-off before it reaches you, one does,
surprisingly, soon stop listening to the roar above you. But it's there, all
day long.

As clearly we are on a class course in smart surroundings, make sure
the leader of this expedition to Catalonia, if you allow him that title, is
dressed for the occasion. Either something classically cut, well-worn but
not too tatty, or discreetly modern, designer-labelled and, therefore,
ludicrously expensive, which will be your perfect excuse for nipping
into Loewe or Gonzalo Comella on *Passeig de Gracia* and treating
yourself to that exclusive outfit you deserve, on his credit card. The
members here are usually suited-up with ties knotted when they go to
the club on weekdays and there is a touch of refined dishevelment about
their attire out on the course, unlike the bedraggled outfits the rest of the
golfing fraternity generally perform in, and most of the lady members
head for the first tee as immaculately attired and groomed as if they
were straight out of an ad for Burberry's.

But your man can relax about his swing; it will probably draw a sigh
of admiration from the starter, accustomed to the quality of his
members' swings which, according to one of amateur golf's general
laws, although with one or two honourable exceptions to the rule, will
be in inverse proportion to the quality of their owner's net worth. Maybe
it is because the well-healed golfer is so dedicated to increasing his
considerable fortune that he has little time to practise. In the case of El
Prat, this observation does not, emphatically, apply to the cadre of
young bloods, with their groomed swings and handicaps of one or
better, which the club always has in its stables and who assure it, year in
and year out, a decent presence in the Spanish national amateur team.

The original layout was opened in 1954, and since then other holes
have been added to bring it to its present thirty-six-hole status. There
are four different courses – green, red, yellow and blue, the longest
being the green course at 5,947 metres (6,504 yards) from the members'
tees. Currently, you are almost always made to play the yellow course,
which measures 5,873 metres (6,422 yards), so this will be the one
described.

It includes the nine most recently constructed holes, which
presumably were designed by an ornithologist with a doctorate in
waterfowl rather than a golfer. The result is acres of marshland lakes,
populated with all sorts of fancy ducks, which get fat feeding on the
thousands of golf balls lying in their stretch of water. Rumour has it that
there is a shop selling surlyn paté somewhere in the area.

The first two holes are innocuous enough and will at least give the golfer the opportunity to bed down his swing for the day before the water festival begins, which it does in a major way at the par five third, with water lying on both sides of the fairway so that the second shot, which would normally be a fairway wood, requires the precision and nerves of a marksman. From the fifth hole on there is no relief from water until you stand, several balls lighter, on the eleventh tee and the respite lasts only one hole because only an outright coward is not going to play the delicate short-iron approach over the water onto the twelfth green; if you go round the side even the ducks laugh. If your man's swing includes a built-in slice he will be lucky to avoid the water waiting to catch his drive on the fourteenth, and he deserves to have his handicap trimmed if he misses the lake and drops his tee-shot on the green at the par three fifteenth, 187 metres (205 yards) away. What water there is on the sixteenth rarely causes a problem so at this point he is virtually home and dry, with only the planes to worry about as they career down at him as he stands on the seventeenth tee.

Someone once said that a club's driving range will tell you all you need to know about the quality of the course itself. At El Prat the driving range is magnificent. Ample, long and flat you always have decent turf to play off and there is room for a legion of players. A green with bunkers and some surrounding fairway for practising green side shots lies just behind.

The course itself, in the twenty or so years this golfer has played it, has never been in anything but championship condition, manicured always to near perfection, a real pleasure to play on, and with palm trees lining many of the fairways and clusters of pine trees alongside others it has an unmistakably Mediterranean look to it. There is, however, a question mark as to the future: the course lies on land leased from the Air Ministry and the airport's next runway will be built right over the fairways of the club. When that will happen and what solution the club will come up with are, today, unknowns.

X X X

This historic and very Mediterranean city has shot up the popularity table of favourite destinations among travellers after its attractions were widely publicized as a by-product of the 1992 Olympic Games, and such is the variety of its appeal that everyone should find something to interest them for a stay of a couple of days or so, although you would need a week to feel it is a town you know. For the traveller flying in to the airport on the coast, as his plane glides down on its final approach there lies this densely built city, laid out on the south-east-facing slope of the Tibidabo, the hill that forms a backdrop to a maze of buildings and streets with a 2,000-year history that crowds right down to the waterfront, and all of it well within your field of vision. What is unusual compared to large cities in northern Europe is that there are virtually no suburbs, and the three million or so inhabitants of the greater metropolitan area are contained in an urban expanse that extends only six kilometres at its widest point and is only about thirteen kilometres long. What facilitates things for the tourist, though, is that most of the interesting places to see are almost all within an area which you can cover on foot although it can make sense to use the Metro for some trips. To enjoy the town you need to walk it, and its ample, tree-lined pedestrian sidewalks, often fifteen metres wide, are designed for just that. Few big cities cater for the pedestrian better than Barcelona.

An attempt to summarize each of the attractions of the city would make tedious reading, and in any case visitors should buy a guide to the town which will list absolutely everything on offer as well as providing a street map and a plan of the Metro. The best place to start your visit is to call in at the Tourist Information Centre at the *Plaça de Catalunya*, where you can quickly update yourself on opening times, current shows and exhibitions, and phone numbers of places where you may wish to reserve a place on a guided tour. This chapter will, then, concentrate on those aspects of the town which are in some way unique to it in the hope that what is briefly described here will encourage you to include at least a couple of days in the town while the golfer puts the courses at El Prat, Sant Cugat and Vallromanes to the test.

A brief, historical outline
Barcelona was founded by the Romans under the emperor Augustus a few years before the birth of Christ although the area had been populated by Iberian tribes, known as the Laietani, as early as the fourth century BC; the Romans named it Barcino, which was an adaptation of the Iberian name of Barkeno. The town was built and populated by Roman legionaries who had earned retirement after campaigns in north-west Iberia. They, as many others since, must have felt that this was a good retirement location, on the same latitude as Rome and so with a

climate to match, and with all the culinary ingredients cultivated locally, including excellent wines, to remind them of home cooking, and the Laietani girls would probably have made good cooks. And, anyway, it was an awfully long march home. Curiously, they made the centre of the town and built the forum, from where the city was governed, in the same place which today, two thousand years later, continues to be the seat of both the city's administration and of the Catalan regional government, the *Plaça Sant Jaume*. The Roman town was quite small, smaller in fact than either Tarraco, the centre of government for the north of the Iberian peninsula, and Empúries on the bay of Roses, but it was the only port, albeit an unprotected one, between Tarraco and Narbonne, and by the beginning of the fourth century the outer city walls reached from a position close to the sea up to the present day cathedral. What remains of these original walls can be seen beside the cathedral and in the Ramón Berenguer square and alongside the *carrer Tapinería*; they are impressively massive and still form part of the buildings since built over them.

The Roman era came to and end with the invasions of the Visigoths at the end of the fourth century, and they held sway for the next three hundred years. Recent archaeological finds reveal that the city grew slowly in this period and that the early Christian Church survived the demise of the Romans and even built a Basilica in the town. The first of the Moorish invasions came in 717 and they stayed until 803, when the city was liberated by Louis the Pious, the king of Aquitaine, the southern part of France, and became part of the Hispanic Marches, an outpost of the Carolingian empire. Even so, in the next 250 years the city suffered several attacks by the Moors, who dominated all of the south of Spain and the Balearic islands, and in 985 the town actually fell to them again, this time to Al-Mansur, the Vizier of Cordoba, although this Moorish presence was short-lived.

Catalonia was by now a nation-state, ruled by the Counts of Barcelona, whose originator, Wilfred the Hairy, had succeeded in imposing his authority on the other Catalan Countships in the ninth century, and had built himself a palace in the town of which no verifiable vestige remains. Henceforth Barcelona would be, and still is, the capital of Catalonia.

The next two centuries were, in architectural terms, the Romanesque period of the town of which very little remains. Under a succession of

Counts of Barcelona, direct descendants of Wilfred the Hairy and all called Berenguer, the town prospered and important buildings were built but only the churches of *Sant Pau del Camp*, the oldest in the city, *Santa Llúcia* and the *Capella de Marcús* survive, and even they are questioned as being genuinely original Romanesque structures. It was, however, a prosperous period in the history of the city, which grew rapidly outside the confines of the walls. Following the union of the Houses of Aragon and the Counts of Barcelona in the twelfth century Catalonia, now a kingdom, expanded its empire quickly and extensively, and Barcelona began a period of growth and prosperity which has hardly been matched since: by 1330 twenty percent of the population of Catalonia lived in the city.

The foundation of the city's prosperity over the next two centuries was trade with other Mediterranean countries and the Near East, hence the increasing importance of the port. It was also a period of feverish construction when palaces, the cathedral, convents, churches and houses for the citizens were built over what had previously been the Romanesque buildings, and this new generation of buildings were Gothic in style. They, substantially, are the core of today's Gothic Quarter and include the *Palau Reial* (Royal Palace) in the *Plaça del Rei*, the church of *El Pi*, the church of *Santa María del Mar* and two impressive halls, *el Saló de Cent* and *el Saló del Tinell*.

The city's fortunes started on a slow but inexorable decline in the fifteenth century brought on by the debilitating sacrifices required to maintain Catalonia's extensive empire in the western Mediterranean, continuing bouts of the mortiferous plague, which hit the town once in each decade in the hundred years after 1360, and a disastrous civil war within the kingdom, which started in 1462. By 1473 the city's economic activity was devastated after Barcelona, which had backed the wrong side in the civil war, fell after a siege and suffered the penal measures imposed on it by the crown. Ferdinand II of Aragon had acceded to the crown of Aragon and Catalonia in 1452, and when he married Isabella of Castilla the court left Barcelona; the royal authority was henceforth represented by a Viceroy appointed by the king, whose residence was also in the *Plaza Reial, El Palacio del Lugarteniente*. To close out the fifteenth century Barcelona witnessed one of history's more memorable events, the reception by the Catholic Monarchs of Christopher Columbus on his return from his voyage of discovery; the exact venue of the event is not known with certainty but it may have taken place in the great hall of the original *Palau Reial.*

In the sixteenth and seventeenth centuries the city hardly grew at all and this explains why there are so few 'Renaissance' buildings in the town although there are two notable exceptions: the *Casa del Arciadá* in the *carrer Santa Llucia* and the façade of the *Generalitat* in the *Plaça Sant Jaume,* which is, in fact, a modification made in the sixteenth century to the original building constructed a hundred years or so earlier. In the Spanish War of Succession, which lasted from 1702 to 1714, Catalonia, egged on by the English, who were as anti-Bourbon as anyone in Europe, sided against the Bourbon pretender, Felipe V. The final outcome was a siege of the town which started in August 1713 and ended on 14 September a year later when the town's garrison, reduced like the rest of the citizens to eating grass, capitulated after the outer walls had been breached. Paradoxically, this cataclysmic defeat, which finally put an end to any degree of independence from Spain, let alone self-government or even the notion that Catalonia's association with Spain was fundamentally voluntary, is now Catalonia's National Day, *la Diada,* celebrated every 14 September. On this day the regional and city authorities ritually visit a sort of Wall of Lament, *el Fossar de les Moreres,* a cemetery where those who died in the defence of the city in 1714 are buried.

Having been put under the yoke of Castille and suffering the indignity of having to house a permanent garrison of Castillian troops, Barcelona set about rebuilding its prosperity with the admirable sense of business pragmatism that has characterized the Catalans ever since. The quarter known as the *Barceloneta* was built and towards the end of the eighteenth century the Rambla was laid out. Meantime, the revival of industry was the work of hundreds of artisans, each employing a few labourers in their workshops, and organized into powerful *Gremios,* the equivalent the London Guilds. Between 1780 and 1797 salaries grew at twice the rate of those in Madrid. One English visitor was notably impressed by a textile factory employing 350 operatives making cloth for the markets in the Americas, and the English economist, Arthur Young, reported hearing 'the noise of business everywhere'; he could make the same remark today and would still be on target.

By the middle of the nineteenth century Barcelona was the industrial capital of Spain and had attracted over 50,000 immigrants from the countryside and other areas of Spain in the space of just eleven years. However, this massive increase in the working-class population, whose rates of pay allowed them little more than a diet of bread and potatoes, garnished occasionally with the odd sardine, produced riot after riot of protest against their miserable situation and the increasing use of steam-driven production machines, which threatened their jobs; every time they were ruthlessly and bloodily repressed, which inevitably left a deep reservoir of resentment. One such incident in 1843, called the *Jamancia*, which, more than a workers' uprising, was an attempt to start a Radical revolution, was repelled by the liberal Bourbon governor, General Espartero, who bombarded the city for thirteen days with cannon from the fort on top of Montjuic, the hill overlooking the harbour and town, and 460 buildings were damaged or destroyed.

But such was the dynamism of the town's economy that it never took long after the latest slaughter for the city authorities to think again in terms of expansion and modernization. Thus in 1859 designs were invited for the expansion of the city, and it was the proposal of the engineer and town planner, Idelfons Cerdà, which was finally chosen, and in 1869 construction of his innovative concept of town planning started. It covers the area of the city between the *Plaça de Catalunya* and the quarter higher up the town called *Gràcia*, and is known as *l'Eixample* (*el Ensanche* in Spanish), meaning the 'expansion'. Apart from a grid layout of the streets, with each intersection bevelled to allow an early vision of traffic crossing in the other direction, the buildings are all of uniform height and all have large courtyards allowing light into the rear side of the apartments; it was radically modern compared to the Gothic Quarter.

The last three decades of the nineteenth century were relatively calm on the socio-political front at least until the 1890s, and the moneyed classes began to enjoy a new lifestyle in the city. Previously, their social life was confined to their houses and the cafés but now, with gas street lighting and a new and elegant area in the town, people were out and about constantly, *Passeig de Gràcia* being the avenue to see and be seen on as opposed to the Rambla, which had previously been the street for displaying one's elegant self in public. This was the period of the revival of a movement to restore a sense of Catalan nationalism, particularly its political and cultural roots, and produced a period of intense creative activity in everything from architecture, art and the letters to craftsmanship and design. In the case of architecture it was, of course, the Moderniste movement. In 1888 Barcelona held its first 'Universal Exhibition', the equivalent of a World Fair, and from here on Barcelona would acquire its international reputation as a dynamic city, a place where the entrepreneurial spirit combined with a methodical approach to work made things happen, distinctly more thrusting, if sometimes a little brash, than the stereotype of Hispanic cultures, generally thought of as lacking any sense of urgency and inclined to live in the comfortable past.

Social turmoil, however, returned in the last decade of the century to explode in the same violent way that it had in the earlier ones. The next episode was to come about with the contagion of anarchism, which, like a new virus of the 'flu, arrived from outside the country, from France in fact. It is difficult from today's perspective to understand how anyone could subscribe to an ideology which, if not preaching virtual chaos as the sublime, social state, at least upheld that all manifestations of order and organization in society were infamous. Their attitudes were often sanctimonious, even puritan at times, which contrasted with the radical anti-clericalism of their political doctrine, which also carried with it a large component of naivety combined with extreme violence and utter intolerance of those who opposed them; but the fact is the anarchist movement captured substantial support in Barcelona, largely among the working class, and it became a political force to be reckoned with up to the end of the 1936-1939 Spanish Civil War. The movement, whose zealous idealists had punctured, literally, the social peace with numerous bomb-throwing incidents in the 1890s, was held responsible for a notorious week of violence in 1909, *la Setmana Tragica* – the Tragic Week. Sparked off by a firebrand, left wing and anti-clerical demagogue, Alejandro Lerroux, a deputy with a large working-class following who called themselves the Young Barbarians, Lerroux, according to Robert Hughes' account, incited his enthusiastic supporters to wreck, in his words, 'this unhappy country... destroy its temples, finish off its gods, tear the veil from its novices and raise them up to be mothers to civilize the species.' So once again, with fury, hatred and without much reflection, the mobs needed no more to indulge in a paroxysm of anti-clericalism. Reportedly, eighty religious buildings, mostly convents, churches, monasteries and even religious schools, were sacked and burned. Mercifully, they did not touch a stone of

Gaudí's *Sagrada Família*, which was already twenty five years into its construction.

Another grand exhibition, the International Exhibition, was held in 1929, which bequeathed the mountain of Montjuich a legacy of stylish, rather grandiose buildings, including the *Palau Nacional*, today the National Museum of Catalan Art, which dominates the Exhibition grounds. This event was a brief respite in the political upheavals that were to lead to the abdication of Alfonso XIII, the establishment of the Republic and, in 1936, the Spanish Civil War, in which the Catalan government, in the form of the *Generalitat*, sided with the Republic against Franco's uprising and so ended on the losing side.

Barcelona under Franco was about as exciting as a dull and gloomy English winter day. It was a period when the heavy hand of centralism in administrative affairs reinforced the regime's repression of anything smacking of Catalan individuality, which to Madrid was synonymous with Catalan independence. It was also a time when public money for investment, not only in new equipment but also for routine maintenance of existing facilities, was virtually at Third World levels and what money there was had to be invested in major, basic infrastructure such as dams across rivers in the mountains to provide water for the population, so that the city gradually slipped down the slope of steady decay to become a rather unkempt provincial town lacking in initiatives and creativity.

The change in the town's fortunes that came about after the death of Franco was simply astonishing. The new, post-Franco Spanish constitution, approved by referendum in 1978, sensibly divided Spain into seventeen autonomous regions, whereby Catalonia among others, which historically enjoyed if not outright independence from Spain at least certain, unique privileges, regained a large measure of self-government, and, of course, town councils were democratically elected and they immediately set out to improve everything they could lay their hands on to make sure they would get reelected next time round. Spain was by now also much richer following the rapid growth of the economy during the sixties and seventies, and all of this brought about a dynamic programme of improvements in the town. Today's flourishing city, spruced up over a period of years in preparation for the 1992 Olympics by a gifted team of local architects, ably led by Oriol Bohigas, and once again a vibrant centre of artistic endeavour, is, perhaps, more handsome than it has ever been throughout its two millennia of turbulent history.

El Modernisme

If there is one feature of Barcelona which singles it out from any other city it is its heritage of Moderniste buildings. Modernisme was the Catalan version of an artistic movement which prevailed in Europe from about 1880 until the early years of the twentieth century, and was known as Art Nouveau in France and England, although there it was also called Modern Style, Jugendstil – 'the style of youth' – in Germany, and in Italy, Liberty, after the store in London, or Floreale. The movement embraced the fine arts, literature, the theatre, and all aspects of design but in Catalonia it would be reflected in architecture and the decorative arts above all else. So great was the impact of this new style on Catalan society that it became a truly popular phenomenon, particularly among the cultured and the wealthy, who immersed themselves in Modernisme to such a degree that its influence as a design trend was evident in everything, from every day, domestic furnishings and fittings to the design of shopfronts, cafés, houses and important public buildings. Like all new fashions, it made what had immediately preceded it look passé, and it was to suffer the same fate when it was succeeded by the next design trend, Noucentisme, meaning the style of the nineteen hundreds. With the exception of the *Sagrada Família* it continued to be thought of as dated and its buildings to be ignored, except by a devoted and admiring minority, until the 1960s, when it recovered its reputation as a remarkable period in architectural design, and the city authorities set about a programme of restoration.

Modernisme in Catalonia also embraced the nationalistic movement, the return to the roots of Catalan culture and its history as an independent state, which was the beacon that the local intellectuals looked to at the time. Every Moderniste building made some sort of reference to the glorious past even if it was only a carving in a stone lintel of St. George, the patron saint of Catalonia, slaying the dragon. And as the decoration of the walls, and, in Gaudí's case, even the roof of a building, was an essential design component in Modernisme, there were always plenty of opportunities to get your nationalistic message across. Unsurprisingly, the architectural expression of Modernismo, as the movement is called in Spanish, never took hold anywhere else in Spain although Gaudí did do some buildings outside Catalonia. Modernismo was, however, an important influence in intellectual circles in Madrid, particularly in literature, a part of the national soul-searching that the loss of what remained of Spain's overseas colonies in 1898 inspired, triggering a turn towards Europe as the compass point for the future.

There were few, clearly defined parameters within the movement to stifle the individual architect's creative ideas on how a building should be designed, which led to quite dramatic differences from one building to another. An example of this is the *'manzana de la discordia'* – the discordant (city) block – on *Passeig de Gracia*, where three buildings on the same block designed by the three most highly rated of the movement's architects, Gaudí, Domènech i Montaner and Puig i Cadalfalch, could hardly be more different. Modernisme was essentially eclectic, happy to seek inspiration from Gothic architecture, which became Neo-Gothicism, or even from Moorish design, and, in the case of Gaudí, whatever came into his extraordinarily fertile, original and fantastical head. This is why visiting these buildings is such an entertaining experience, they are all so rich in detail and different, not only between architects but also between buildings by the same architect. The Moderniste building, however, was not just a case of stylish design within the genre: the architect relied heavily on the skills of artisans from different trades who were to execute, and often contribute, design ideas to the decoration of the building, a key feature in a Moderniste project; every building required highly skilled craftsmen from many specialist trades. Ceramics, gold and silver work, wrought ironwork, stained glass and furniture making were all essential trades in the process of the execution of a project, so much so that without them a Moderniste building would have been impossible. This aspect of the formula also made for massive costs, which sometimes obliged even the richest of patrons, such as Eusebi Guëll, finally to throw in the towel as he did before the Parque Guëll could be completed. Never since has building been able to contemplate such idiosyncratic and prohibitively costly design concepts but buildings since have never attempted to give you a work of art in the design and the decoration of their structural elements and the outer weathering skin. After visiting a Gaudí building you feel the sort of elation you would after viewing a multi-discipline exhibition of the arts.

The city's tourist office have made it easy to set about the task of immersing yourself in Modernisme by recently introducing what they call *La ruta del Modernisme*, the Modernisme route. As the details of this are likely to change as a result of practical experience it is advisable to check with the Tourist Information Centre in the *Plaça de Catalunya* for the latest details but currently you can buy a visitor's ticket, which gets you into ten different buildings for Ptas 1,500, and furthermore includes guided tours in English at certain times of the day in several of them, and a guided tour is always worth five unguided ones. You are also given some good documentation on fifty different places, most of them Moderniste buildings, associated with the movement and a street map which traces a route to follow on foot to some of the key buildings.

If you have the time and interest in Modernisme you should try to visit at least eight locations, three of which are almost adjacent to each other on the 'discordant (city) block'. Several of these buildings have been declared part of 'The Heritage of Humanity' by Unesco. The *Palau Guëll* (the Guëll Palace), a substantial town house built just off La Rambla for the Guëll family, *la Casa Batlló* and *la Casa Milà* (popularly known as *La Pedrera*), both on *Passeig de Gràcia*, the *Sagrada Família* and the *Parque Guëll* were all designed by Gaudí. *El Palau de la Música Catalana*, a concert hall, and *la Casa Lleó Morera*, the second of the trio in the 'discordant block', were designed by Lluís Domenèch i Montaner, who, if you exclude Gaudí from the movement and some experts do maintaining that he was altogether too original to be included with the rest, was the most brilliant of the Moderniste architects. The last of the eight recommended visits, and the third of the 'discordants' is *la Casa Amatller*, designed by Josep Puig i Cadalfach when he was only twenty one. If time is short, the *Sagrada Família* is the most impressive of all the Moderniste buildings, the *Palau de la Música Catalana* is outstanding, and the four buildings on *Passeig de Gracia* can be viewed at least from the outside whenever you happen to walk along this stylish avenue, with both *La Casa Milà* and *La Casa Batlló* illuminated at night. While at the *Sagrada Família* you can see another splendid example of Moderniste architecture just up the *Avinguda Gaudí*, the *Hospital de la Santa Creu i Sant Pau*, designed by Domenèch i Montaner, and still a hospital today.

Antoni Gaudí
Antoni Gaudí is the most famous of all the Moderniste architects and he was also the most original. Born in the town of Reus in 1852 and the son of a boilermaker, he studied at the School of Architecture in Barcelona

Antoni Gaudí (centre). Arxiu històric, Ajuntament de Barcelona.

64

from 1873 to 1877. Gaudí laid great importance on the fact that he had grown up in a family of artisans, where he watched his father fashion complex shapes out of sheet metal with his hands, a trade that then had more to do with an instinctive and empirical approach to producing the end product than a precise process following minutely detailed drawings. And that was the method Gaudí was to use in creating his buildings, full of daring, geometrical shapes with difficult, intricate transitions. At the school of architecture he was taught conventional, linear, two-dimensional construction drawing in which plan, elevation and cross sections depict the components and method of construction of a building; this is not at all suited to the rendering of the undulating irregular forms that he used, and throughout his life he produced drawings sparingly, preferring to make three-dimensional models on site to explain to the craftsmen and construction crews what they were to make.

Any patron who commissioned him to do a building needed a large capacity for swallowing quite radical changes in the design as a project progressed because Gaudí worked much like an intuitive sculptor, whose final inspiration for the next part of an abstract composition comes only after he has completed the previous section. In *La Pedrera*, you can see the official drawings, signed by the building owner, Pere Milà, by Gaudí as the project architect and by the Town Architect, which were submitted to the municipal authorities to obtain a building permit: it depicts a building quite different in appearance from the one actually built!

Gaudí was a gifted and polyvalent designer but he was also an excellent building technician, capable of introducing novel, structural forms which were highly efficient. It is one thing to dream up extravagant, geometrical shapes but without the practical, construction techniques for their execution they would have remained no more than fantasies, at best visualized in a model. His design abilities, apart from the strictly architectural, embraced wrought ironwork, cast iron, furniture, mosaics, ceramics and innumerable forms of *trencadis*, the decoration of surfaces with fragments of tile or glass. This decorative technique, first used by the Moors, is a hallmark of Gaudí's buildings and he used it time and again, often resorting to unlikely materials such as fragments of green glass from broken wine bottles or even blue–grey, vitrified limestone from the linings of lime kilns, but the effect was always dazzling.

His inspiration for the unusual forms he designed into his buildings came principally from nature. He had always been an observant youngster and any striking feature from the local countryside was locked away in his mind to be recalled when working on a project. He maintained that nature was 'the Great Book, always open, that we should force ourselves to read.' Plants and the human body were the two most valuable sources of ideas from nature, and he was intrigued by the structure of plants. In the *Sagrada Família* thirty species of plant feature in the stonework but often he would design building elements, such as columns, in stone but looking just as if they were leaning tree trunks or a fibrous cypress tree. Even the hyperbolic or catenary arch was, he observed, just like the shape between two fingers of the hand spread apart.

As you visit some of his buildings what causes an impact, apart from the aesthetic pleasure of the designs of an internationally recognized master, is that the buildings are still in everyday use even though they may be under Unesco's patronage. *La Pedrera* was built for Sr Milà as an investment as well as his own home. Like the other large quality apartment blocks in *l'Eixample*, the first floor was the home of the owner, all 1,200 square metres of it, with a separate and more luxurious staircase leading up to it from the entrance hall. The other floors were each divided into four flats of about 300 square metres which he would rent out, and access to them was by a separate staircase. The contracts that Pere Milà signed with the first tenants included a clause which would allow up to four generations of the family to have first refusal for renewing the lease, and there are still direct descendants of the original families living in the building which today is owned by one of the large Catalan savings banks. The bank has undertaken a major restoration programme of the building, which now is in pristine condition, and has installed what is the largest exhibition of the life and works of Gaudí on the top floor. The visit to the roof-terrace is a must to view the extraordinary forms Gaudí gave to the ventilator shafts and chimneys, looking like some powerful drawn and twisted creatures from a grotesque world, patrolling the Barcelona sky with expressionless eyes from under a warrior's helmet.

The interiors of the apartments in the Casa Batlló and the *Pedrera* are as undulating as the exteriors. The ceilings swirl like whipped cream and the walls hardly have a straight line on them, which is why Gaudí designed curling furniture moulded to the walls and corners. One tenant in the the *Pedrera* asked Gaudí where on earth was she to put her piano, to receive in reply the suggestion that she could take up the violin.

La Sagrada Família

This best known of all his work was to be Gaudí's consuming passion for forty three years, from 1883, when he was appointed as the architect, until 1926, when he died at the age of 74, still a bachelor, after being run down by a tram. The project was the child of a lay association, the Josephines, who were part of the Church's response to the threat that political Liberalism represented to the faith; a new impulse to revive the devotion to the Holy Family was called for, and this lay group's full title defined devotion to St Joseph, hence the name Josephines, as its spiritual inspiration. The group acquired a block of land on the outskirts of *l'Eixample*, and after a false start with another architect chose Gaudí to replace him for, it seems, his piety, and indeed there never was any question about his devout Catholicism. He was charged with construction of the Expiatory Temple of the Sacred Family, which was never contemplated as a cathedral because Barcelona already had one.

The crypt is the original architect's design, and is Neo-Gothic in style. Gaudí changed little of this. The first major unit to be built which reflected his unmistakable originality was the façade of the Nativity facing almost although not truly due east, which Gaudí would have preferred, but the crypt he had inherited limited his freedom to orientate the building. With its four bell towers of unusual shape and topped by spires brightly coloured in *trencadis*, and the dense profusion of figures, plants and animals, a litany of pre- and post-Christian iconography and symbolism carved in the stonework, this is a façade of a major church like no other. Gaudí used different sculptors to carve the figures but it was he who decided what went where, even choosing the human models to be sculpted. To appreciate the wealth of detail you should take small field glasses with you when you visit.

On the opposite side is the façade of the Passion, which Gaudí did not even see start because throughout the construction of the *Sagrada Família* in his lifetime finance, or rather the lack of it, was the brake that slowed construction to a crawl and at times brought it to a halt. He did, however, leave quite detailed conceptual drawings of what the façade was to be, and from these subsequent construction has continued, and it can be viewed today close to its final form. The bell towers mirror those of the Nativity but the whole area which forms the portico is a dramatic expression of aching, racked humanity on the cross, the fine, inclined columns of the atrium looking just like human bones with taughtened sinews running up them. Gaudí was depicting what he saw as the supreme sacrifice of the crucifixion.

The construction of the temple has continued to the present day, financed by donations, some of the most generous of which come from Japan where Gaudí's work is much admired, and the project is now controlled by an independent trust fortunately free of political interests and of an independence of mind such that even declamations from the purist school of architects, who oppose any continuation of the building because it will never be quite like Gaudí would have done it, do not appear to have a chance of deterring them from seeing the project through, maybe in another fifty years from now. And Gaudí insisted often that, above all else, he wanted the building to be finished.

El Palau de la Música Catalana

This concert hall, built for the Barcelona choral society, *El Orfeó Català*, is a place to intoxicate the eye and the ear. Whether you are a music lover or not, the way to enjoy this building is to attend a performance and combine the pleasures of the music with the heady enjoyment of the hall's exuberant decoration. Finished in 1908, it is considered a jewel of Barcelona's Modernisme together with Gaudí's *Casa Milà*. It is very difficult to get tickets for a performance unless you book months ahead through your travel agent but you can visit the building most days of the week as part of the Moderniste tour, and this is one site where a guide is essential for you to understand and appreciate the rich details in the design. The interior of the building will stay long in your memory.

El Barrio Gótico

The Gothic Quarter of Barcelona is one of Europe's most important assemblages of buildings from the thirteenth, fourteenth and fifteenth centuries in a major city. The name 'Gothic Quarter' was only attributed to it quite recently, and it is also referred to as the *Casc Antic*, the old part, *la ciutat vella* – the old city – and even the *Barrio Judio*, which is just one part of it. Not everyone agrees on its precise limits, some maintaining that it covers the area only of the old, walled city, and others enlarging its extent to the east of *Via Laietana* to include the unquestionably Gothic buildings of the church of *Santa María del Mar* and most of what lies on the *carrer Montcada*. To confuse the visitor further, the *Barrio Chino*, historically the Red Light district, borders on the Rambla, which does constitute part of the *Barrio Gótico* while the *Barrio Chino* does not. All that is worth seeing from this period in the city's history in fact lies (taking the axis of La Rambla as running north-south for this exercise) south of the *Plaça de Catalunya* down to the port, east of La Rambla and west of the *Mercat del Born*, the old fruit and vegetable market. The only building outside these limits is the *Drassanes*, the mediaeval shipyard, which lies scarcely one block west of the bottom of La Rambla.

A very good option for visiting the *Barrio Gótico* is to take one of the English language guided walks, which are currently organized every day except Monday in the mornings and afternoons. There are guided walks also in French and German on certain days. For this book, rather than construct several routes to follow, it seems more appropriate to comment on streets and buildings and let you mark in on a street map where to go to see whatever appeals to you.

Unless your base for your stay is somewhere in the *Barrio Gótico*, your starting point for a stroll through the Barrio's streets would either be the *Plaça de Catalunya* or the port end of La Rambla, and several lines of the Metro converge on the *Plaça de Catalunya* if that is your choice, or you can make the Metro station of *Drassanes* on Line 3 the place to start, down at the bottom of La Rambla.

La Rambla

At some stage in your stay you must stroll the length of Barcelona's most famous old street. Few, if any, streets in the world deserve the description of 'cosmopolitan' more than La Rambla, which seethes with humanity round the clock, a social mix of classes, nationalities and races. It drops down from the *Plaça de Catalunya* to the port, bordered by cafés, shops, old apartments and churches, and, in the central walkway under the plane trees, flower and bird stalls gradually give way to pavement café tables and then one-man stalls selling trinkets and bits of almost anything to the visitors to the city. Originally, it was a river bed skirting the mediaeval walls, and was first paved in the eighteenth century. It is not in any way beautiful: its appeal is simply its vibrant atmosphere and the changing pastiche of scenes as you walk along. Although commonly called La Rambla or Las Ramblas for its entire length, its name changes as it drops down to the port: Rambla de Canaletas at the top, then successively Rambla dels Estudis, Rambla de les Flors, Rambla dels Capuxins, and finally Rambla de Sta Monica. All these names come from associations with buildings flanking the street in the past, many of them convents. At the top end, round the Canaletas water font, rows of chairs line both sides of the central walkway, from where the locals and anyone else who fancies contemplating the scene sit and review the passing of humanity, merchant sailors from Russia to Korea, making their way up from the port to the centre of the town, students, tourists, local folk who live around La Rambla, the occasional businessman, latter-day hippies, who find all this something close to a state of nirvana, and representatives of just about every race under the sun, all ambling along under the trees.

Buildings to watch out for as you descend La Rambla towards the sea start with the *Farmàcia Nadal* at no. 121, with a Moderniste shopfront decorated in mosaics, and then *El Palau de la Virreina* at no. 99, built in 1778 and named after the Viceroy of Peru's young wife, whose husband had married her at the age of seventy two but who did not survive the seven years' construction of the palace he was building for his retirement so it was named after the attractive young widow, *La Virreina*, and now houses art exhibitions. The *St José* market at no. 91, commonly called the *Boqueria*, and once included by *Life* magazine in a list of the ten best markets in the world, is an experience not to be missed. You walk through the Moderniste entrance and then drift slowly round inside, observing the superbly presented fruit and vegetable stalls, each displaying a minor work of art which it seems a pity to spoil by actually buying anything, and then move on to the fish stalls, where the variety of fish on offer will catch your eye but not to the extent of blinding you to the ladies selling them, all got up as gorgeously as if they had just emerged from a beautician's, including those rather long in the tooth, and wearing what you might mistake for titillating night dresses but are in fact frilly aprons, and all determined not to be outshone by that peroxide little vixen in the stall next door who has been undercutting the price of prawns for the last month in attempt to attract someone else's clients. Another rich, Moderniste shopfront is *Antiga Casa Figueres* at no. 83, today a pastry shop, and a little lower down on the same side of the street the *Café de la Òpera*, which opened in 1929 and always looks as though it hasn't had a decent spring clean since, perhaps because it has preserved its original furniture and some eighteenth-century-style mirrors, with opera-inspired female figures etched onto the glass. It is usually close to being full at most times of the day but you will enjoy a coffee in its 1920s ambience.

Almost opposite the *Café de la Òpera* is the site of the Barcelona opera house, *El Liceu*, opened in 1847 and burned to the ground for the second time in its history in 1994, and currently under reconstruction with an expected opening date early in 1999. The renovated theatre will be adorned with all the Baroque trimmings of the original which made it such a stylish amphitheatre. The sixty-metre-tall statue of Christopher Columbus marks the southern end of La Rambla, with the man himself pointing, arm outstretched, in a direction which is anything but west. You can take a lift inside the column for a crow's-nest view of the town.

The word Rambla crops up in many Catalan towns and always refers to some kind of walkway. Heading uphill out of one corner of the *Plaça de Catalunya* is the *Rambla de Catalunya*, one of the most elegant streets in *l'Eixample*, with a wide, central walkway full of café tables in the warmer months. It is not, however, part of La Rambla as such.

Club de Golf Sant Cugat

This is the oldest course in Catalonia, founded by English residents in the area in 1914. Originally a nine-hole course, it was enlarged in the sixties to its present eighteen-hole status; it is a short but enjoyable layout in the town of Sant Cugat, today virtually a dormitory suburb of Barcelona and within easy access from there by car through the Valvidrera tunnel, and by rail from any of the stations of the *Ferrocariles de Catalunya*, which connect with the Barcelona Metro system and take you right into town of Sant Cugat.

In golfing terms this course is rather tame, measuring only 5,214 metres (5,702 yards) for a par of seventy. It has one longish par five, the eighteenth, at 457 metres (500 yards) but on the par fours one seldom has to play more than a short iron for the second shot, and for the long hitters some greens on the par fours are driveable. The character of the course is similar to an English park land layout, the fairways often running alongside each other with just some trees separating one from another. There are a few gentle slopes to negotiate but, except for one notoriously steep par three, nicknamed 'the heart attack' by the members, nothing that could really be called a hill. At certain vantage points there are good views of the Montserrat and Montensy mountains, those two symbols of the homeland so deeply entrenched in the Catalan collective psyche. It is an ideal venue for those who do not want a severe examination of their golf or of their physical fitness, and the fact is that Club de Golf San Cugat is popular with players from all over Catalonia, even more so since the standard of course maintenance has reached a new peak in recent years.

The doyen of Catalan golf has a clubhouse befitting its senior status. The original clubhouse was a small, pokey little masia, whose main virtues were its age and authenticity. When the course was remodelled in the sixties the club also enlarged the clubhouse and the architect achieved what so many of his profession do with old buildings in Spain – a remarkable symbiosis of the original building, subtly adapted inside, and a modern but tasteful extension to provide additional space for the reception area, changing rooms and the club's administration offices. It is now a very appealing clubhouse, just the right size to accommodate the numerous membership without giving you the feeling that you're in something the size of an airport terminal. And the bar is the snuggest in the region.

X X X

La Plaça Reial

A little further down La Rambla from *El Liceu* and on the other side of the street is the porticoed rectangular *Plaça Reial*, the Royal Square, surrounded on all sides by a rather formal façade of apartments giving it something of the character of French buildings of the Napoleonic period on which it was indeed modelled, and it is the only square in the city to have been designed as a complete unit. Built in the middle of the nineteenth century, it was intended to be an attractive housing project for the moneyed, middle classes. However, by the 1880s these had moved out to the new *Eixample* and from then on the *Plaça Reial* went downhill until a century later when the Town Council renovated the exterior of the buildings, spruced up the square itself and placed more or less permanent police patrols inside to ensure that the drug peddlers, whose out-of-doors market it had become, moved out. Since then it has become a semi-fashionable place for intellectuals to live although they do so with a colourful cross-section of society as neighbours. For the visitor it is a good place to sit out, sheltered from whatever wind may be blowing, have a drink and admire the two Gaudí, six-lamp, cast-iron street lights, designed when he was only twenty seven. There are several beer establishments under the arches where students traditionally celebrate the end of the academic year until the small hours, and on Sunday mornings a well attended stamp and coin market occupies the square.

La Plaça Sant Jaume

This square is in the heart of the area with the oldest buildings in the Gothic quarter, and you can walk to it from La Rambla on the *carrer Ferran*, which is the street bordering the *Plaça Reial* on its north side, or you can approach it from the *Plaça de Catalunya* by walking down the *Portal de l'Angel*, which leads on to the *carrer Cucurull* and from there down the *carrer Arce* and into the *Plaça de la Catedral*. From here you can choose either of the two, narrow little streets that run up beside the cathedral, the *carrer del Bisbe* and the *carrer de Sant Honorat*. At the most it will take you ten minutes from the *Plaça de Catalunya* provided you don't stop to look at other sights on the way. The nearest Metro station is *Jaume I* on Line 4.

The *Plaça Sant Jaume* is where the Roman Forum was sited and it continues today as the seat of local government, the *Palau de la Generalitat* with its Renaissance façade housing the regional government, and across the square is the Town Hall and its nineteenth-century Neo-Classical frontage although the origins of the building date back to the fifteenth century. Together, they make an impressive architectural statement of the dignity of government institutions, a reassurance for citizens disillusioned by the banality if not the venality of some of their political representatives. With these two substantial buildings forming the backdrop to the cobbled square the overall effect is one of classic elegance and spaciousness, a striking contrast to the narrow shaded streets of most of the Gothic quarter.

El Palau de la Generalitat. Arxiu històric, Ajuntament de Barcelona.

El Palau de la Generalitat

The institution of the *Generalitat* dates back to 1359, when the Catalan parliament, *Les Corts*, which since 1300 were seen to represent the 'totality' or 'generality' of Catalonia, hence the name *'Generalitat'*, appointed a number of deputies to the permanent commission of the 'Generality' to administer certain extraordinary taxes. By the beginning of the fifteenth century the *Generalitat* had already assumed part of the royal prerogative and carried out the decisions of the Catalan parliament; in 1403 two buildings were purchased to house it, and modifications and improvements were carried out over the next thirty six years to cater for the growing number and importance of its functions. This original mediaeval building, the small central core of today's *Palau*, is one of the few in Europe from this period which is still used for the role for which it was originally designed.

Under the present arrangements you can only visit the building by prearranged appointment on Saturday mornings with a guide – the building is, of course, the executive offices of the president of the regional government so daily groups of tourists would interfere with official business. It is well worth a visit, which your hotel can arrange by phone, to see its splendid rooms and chambers, including the tiny chapel of *Sant Jordi* finished in 1439, the wide stone staircase leading up to the Gothic gallery, which forms a finely proportioned cloister built in 1425 with the slimmest marble columns supporting its Gothic arches, and then the standard media showcase for political encounters today, *el Pati dels Tarongers*, the 'Patio the Orange Trees', which is a roof terrace open to the sky with a few orange trees planted in a formal pattern. The *Saló de Sant Jordi*, a large domed reception chamber originally built as a chapel at the beginning of the sixteenth century, is used today for solemn political and cultural functions: if you have never been invited to attend anything here you are still a nobody in Catalan life. The sixteenth century *Saló Daurat*, the Golden Salon, and the *Sala Torres Garcia*, an eighteenth-century chamber, are two more handsome rooms in an imposing ensemble of historic buildings, and what adds to their appeal is that they are not just museum pieces but are still in daily practical use. Before moving on elsewhere take a look at the original fifteenth-century entrance to the mediaeval building, which is in the *carrer Bisbe*, with its pinnacles and a medallion of Sant Jordi decoratively carved into the stone cornice of the wall.

After your visit to the *Palau Sant Jordi* you may feel like a coffee or even something stronger: there is a pleasant, unfussy little chocolate bar on the right hand corner of the *Plaça Sant Jaume* as you face the *Palau de la Generalitat* or you can cross the square to the *Plaça Sant Miquel* just below the Town Hall where *El Paraigua*, a modern comfortable and stylish little cafeteria will provide you with anything from coffee to *cava*.

If your legs are still game and your historical curiosity still intact you can walk across the *Plaça de Sant Jaume* on any Saturday or Sunday from 10 a.m. until 2 p.m. and visit the Town Hall, *La Casa de la Ciutat* or *La Casa Gran* as it is also called. There are guided tours every hour but you will have to check at which times of the day the tour is in English. The Gothic-style façade which gives on to the *carrer Ciutat* was built by Arnau Bargues and completed in 1402. Inside, the main attraction is the *Saló de Cent*, built in 1373 to house the deliberations of the *Consell de Cent*, a council of, nominally, one hundred citizens elected annually by a collegiate group consisting of the Mayor, five deputies and the chief magistrate to run the city's affairs; these in turn were chosen annually by the Council itself to select its composition for the following year, which must have made for some furious mutual back-scratching. Its origin was in the reign of Jaume I and it endured nearly 450 years, a remarkable record in a European context, until it was abolished after the fall of Barcelona to the Castillian troops of Felipe V in 1714 – that Armageddon of Catalan history. The *Saló de Cent* itself was inaugurated in 1373, a wide high chamber with four arches carrying the wooden roof beams. It has a comfortable, institutional look to it that is unusual from an age when practically all monumental building was ecclesiastical.

From the *Plaça de Sant Jaume* down to the Cathedral Avenue, no more than a few hundred metres, lies a rich congestion of mediaeval buildings for the visitor to consume at whatever pace and in the order that most appeal to him or her. They are all contained within a rectangle formed by the *Via Laietana* to the east, the *Plaça de Sant Jaume* to the south and the Avenue of the Cathedral to the north and the *carrer Sant Honorat* to the west.

La Plaça del Rei

This small square, on summer evenings often the venue for open air concerts, contains a rich collection of mediaeval buildings and the chance for indulging in an exceptional historical experience, a visit to the remains of the Roman city excavated from under the existing mediaeval buildings and cleverly presented as an archaeological site that a visitor can tour in comfort. To achieve this, some major engineering has had to be done to hold up the buildings above but the result amply justifies the effort, and this is another case of the advisability of joining a guided tour through these archaeological finds to get the most out of your visit. It is best to start your visit in the *Museo de Historia de la Ciutat*, which is also the starting point for the archaeological tour and which is housed in the *Casa Clariana Padèllas*, a fifteenth-century building which belonged to a noble family and which was moved stone by stone from its original site in the *carrer Mercaders* to this location in the *Plaça del Rei*. A tour of the rooms takes you through the history of the city from Roman times to the nineteenth century. All forming part of the same museum are the other buildings in the *Plaça del Rei*. The *Palau Reial Major* at the back of the square was originally the residence of the Counts of Barcelona and later became the residence of the Catalo-Aragon kings. Originally built in 1162 by Ramón Berenguer IV it was continually modified down the centuries and perhaps the most interesting part of it is the *Saló del Tinell*, built by Pere III's architect, Guillem Carbonell, and finished midway through the fourteenth century; this is one of the widest buildings, with a span of fifty five feet, ever built in Europe using a structure of unreinforced masonry arches. Its name means a banqueting hall but it was also for a time the parliament building and it may have been the hall where the Catholic Monarchs received Christopher Columbus on his return from his voyage of discovery. It is used today for official meetings and banquets.

Inside the same building you can visit the chapel of *Santa Agueda*. Built by Jaume II and in fine condition today, this was the royal chapel. It has a notable polychromatic wooden ceiling and a marvellous altar-piece by Jaume Huguet, exquisite in detail and well conserved. As the church was built right against the Roman wall you can go out on a part of it, nine metres high and over three and a half metres thick. One of the defensive watch towers, which were part of the wall and spaced out at ten-metre intervals, has been reconstructed to give a real idea of how the wall looked.

On the left hand side of the square stands the *Palau del Lloctinent*, known also as *Palau dels Virreis*, the Viceroys' Palace, for whom it was built by the *Generalitat* in the sixteenth century after the court had left Barcelona, and today is the official archive of the Middle Ages. Inside, the most striking architectural features are a fine Italianate domed ceiling over the main staircase and the Renaissance-style interior patio.

The Cathedral

The present-day cathedral was built over an earlier Romanesque basilica which covered approximately the same area and whose only remains are the chapel of *Santa Llucía* on the street of the same name just beside the cathedral. Construction of the cathedral itself started in 1298 in the reign of Jaume II and continued until 1454 although the main façade which faces on to the *Avinguda de la Catedral*, was not finished in its present form until the end of the nineteenth century; the architects responsible for its completion followed the original design of Maestro Carli, who had detailed it in 1408, but the patina of centuries is missing.

It is unquestionably an important building in the Gothic style but it does have some characteristics that differentiate from other such monuments. It is unusually dark inside and rather sombre, in part because the side walls give on to a series of chapels whose windows are right at the back so that the light reaching the main nave is tenuous unless the interior illumination is on, which you need to appreciate the proportions and impressive height of the building. There are some highly ornate altar-pieces in the side chapels, and the choir and pulpit are also beautifully designed and executed in wood. Under the main altar is the crypt of *Santa Eulàlia*, the patron saint of Barcelona, with a sarcophagus in alabaster sculpted in 1327.

Before leaving the cathedral precincts you should visit the cathedral cloister, which you access from the *carrer Pietat*, and which is considered one of the jewels of the *Barrio Gótico*. The cloister encloses a small garden with a fountain, palm trees, medlar trees and magnolia, and even some geese and pigeons, all of which generates an atmosphere of calm and, in the height of the summer, coolness. It's a good place to find somewhere to sit and rest those aching feet.

To one side of the entrance to the cathedral is the *Casa de la Canonja*, built in 1450 for a charity, *La Pía Almoina*, founded in 1009 originally to provide meals for one hundred poor every day. On the other side of the cathedral and built on the original Roman wall with three of its towers still intact is the *Casa de l'Ardiaca*, the Archdeacon's house, which is today the city's historical archive.

Antiques and la Plaça del Pi

If you are a collector or just someone who enjoys poking about in antique shops the *carrer Palla* which runs from the square in front of the cathedral to the *Plaça Josep Oriol* adjacent to *Plaça del Pi*, will interest you. This is the street of antique shops, an opportunity for a pleasant meander if not a credit-card-waving orgy, which leaves you in the *Plaça del Pi*, literally the 'Pine Tree' square, one of the *Barrio Gótico's* most attractive little corners, usually full of life and with something of a bohemian air to it. It is dominated by the fourteenth-century church of *Santa María del Pi*, built in the soberest of Gothic styles and a major example of the Golden Age of mediaeval construction in Barcelona; today it presides over all that goes on in the square, from street musicians entertaining the clients at the streetside tables of the bars to artists exhibiting their work at the weekends. There always seems to be a holiday atmosphere in the air especially in the late afternoon and early evening. If the idea of staying in a hotel right in the centre of the Gothic quarter appeals you could do worse than book a room in the economical two star Hotel Jardí (phone 93-3015900), which gives on to the *Plaça del Pi*.

El carrer Petritxol

Starting in one corner of the *Plaça del Pi* this short diminutive street connects the *Plaça* with the *carrer Ferran*, that main artery between La Rambla and the *Plaça Sant Jaume. Petritxol*, though, is something special. It is populated on both sides at ground-floor level by small shops, art galleries – including the *Sala Parés*, where all the celebrated Catalan painters since 1884 have exhibited, including Picasso, Rusiñol and Llimona – and a few *Granjas*, a mix of café and pastry shop which are very popular with Barcelonans for an afternoon snack or on Sunday mornings the traditional *suizo*, a cup of hot chocolate with cream and a doughy local pastry called *ensaimada*. The higher floors of the buildings are still apartments. The local shopkeepers have put up illustrated tiled maxims on the outside walls to inform and occasionally edify the passer-by; it is narrow and busy and entertaining, ideal for a stroll and, why not, a *suizo*, and it is just fifty metres long.

Club de golf Vallromanes

This course has a clubhouse you simply must not miss. Originally the family seat of the Taverners, Counts of Darnius, this impressive stone-built mansion, emblazoned with family portraits in ceramic tiles on the exterior of its main façade, was built in 1718 overlooking the narrow valley winding past the village of Vallromanes up into the thickly-wooded slopes of the western side of the coastal hills separating the districts of El Maresme and El Vallés Oriental. Regardless of which direction you are coming from you can reach the club either by exiting the A-7 motorway at Granollers or by exiting the A-19 motorway at Alella, and head for the village of Vallromanes on the BP-5002; the trip will take you only thirty minutes from central Barcelona and a little more from Girona.

When the club was founded in 1968 this old palace with a tiny family chapel adjacent to the main building, was a virtual ruin but under the gifted direction of Sr Ros de Ramis, the architect commissioned to restore and adapt it to the needs of the club, by 1972 it had been reconditioned and enlarged to make it the most impressive of all the clubhouses in Catalonia. Even for a club with close to a thousand members there is a sense of ample space inside that surprises you – and a substantial area of the building is reserved for children's activities and so is not seen by the visitor.

As you park your car in the parking area alongside a forty-metre-long, low building which looks just like racing stables at Newmarket, you might think that perhaps the club also keeps a string of thoroughbreds as well as providing golf for its members but, in fact, this is just part of the store for golf carts. With facilities like these the visiting golfer's sense of anticipation of what the course has in store for him will already be at the adrenalin-drenching level.

And this is the question a course with a clubhouse as fine as this one has to answer: does the course do justice to the clubhouse?

While you might decide to enjoy a lazy four hours in these manorial surroundings, which include a large swimming pool in a secluded garden area as well as tennis and paddle courts, rather than investigate, for example, El Maresme, the Wizard of the Wedge will be straining at the leash to put this course, designed by Frank Hawtree and opened in 1972, to the test. The practice tee is kept in acceptable condition thanks to the heroic efforts of the attendant who manages to keep most of it green through the summer months even though, apart from the tee area, no grass was ever sown on the rest of the range. The first tee of a dog-leg par four will tempt the longer hitters to cut the corner over some trees but a 200-metre tee-shot kept to the centre/left of the fairway opens up the large two-level green totally protected by bunkers; anything short and right off the tee is penalized by trees on the second shot. The view facing the player as he sets up the shot to the green is repeated on seven of the next eight holes, bunkers remorselessly protecting the front of the greens obliging the player to land his ball on the putting surface or be condemned to the sand. The club had the first nine greens completely remodelled in 1997 and the result is large undulating greens with landscaped rough surrounding them, and all of them heavily bunkered. The outward nine are more difficult and better for it although the new greens, at the end of their first year, are still on the slow side.

The first nine holes were laid out in a wider section of the valley and run parallel to each other but there is still adequate variety between one hole and another. The par four third is probably the most testing of these holes, requiring an accurate shot to the long but narrow green. The view from the elevated tee of the short par four fifth offers an eye-catching panorama typical of the rest of the course, the heavily-wooded steep hills surrounding the valley forming the horizon wherever you look, a truly rural setting only a stone's throw from the big Metropolis. The one eyesore on the outward nine which cried out for a solution during the first twenty five years history of the club, an open storm drain shedding water off the surrounding hills, has recently been tidied up.

The ninth green is lodged right under the clubhouse and the tenth tee bang in front of it. This is the stroke index 1 hole, a 402 metre (440 yard) par four played from an elevated tee to a large flat green, the pattern for most of the greens on the inward nine which have not been altered from Hawtree's original design. The course works its way up the ever narrower valley, climbing quite steeply from the eleventh green to the tee of the fourteenth but without exhausting the player, and no two holes are alike. The tee-shot on the fifteenth will, to put it mildly, displease the higher handicap player, two large pines blocking out the entire fairway just as if someone had built a fifteen-metre-high wall across the fairway at about the 150 metre mark from the tee which virtually converts this 338 metre (370 yard) par four into a par five for most of the members; one wonders what the outcome would be if a referendum was held among them to decide if those two pines should be removed. The 367 metre (401 yard) eighteenth is a handsome finishing hole with an elevated green tucked right under those racing stables.

The course was host to the Spanish open won by Seve Ballesteros in 1985 and has also featured on the LPGA tour. With the new greens it has definitely improved as a test of golf since then but has been plagued for too many years by sub-standard course maintenance, the result of unwise choices in the selection of a succession of greenkeepers. At the time of writing a new American-trained greenkeeper has been taken on board and the condition of the course is, currently, as good as the top five or so in the region. If these standards are maintained Vallromanes while not being so severe a test of golf as, say, Pals, Bonmont or Empordà, is unquestionably a course to play and, excusing a few ragged details like the bunkers on the second nine with the consistency of a tennis clay court, yes, it does do justice to its splendid clubhouse.

✗ ✗ ✗

Santa María del Mar

You can approach this outstanding work of Gothic design, considered by some to be the best piece of architecture in the city, either from the *Passeig del Born* which starts close to the *Estación de Francia* or from the port area where the *Passeig Colom* becomes the *Passeig Isabell II*, just by the *Llotja de Mar* with its Neo-Classical exterior built over the original Gothic construction and which until recently housed the Barcelona Stock Exchange and at one time the Barcelona School of Fine Arts, where Picasso studied. The *carrer Camvis Vell* takes you from *La Llotja* to the church of *Santa Maria del Mar.*

What first impresses as you enter the church through the main door is the absolute simplicity of the interior, unadorned columns soaring up to the vaulted roof, the purest of Gothic design with beautifully balanced proportions and free from any detracting additions by later generations. It was built in the fourteenth century and, as the period of construction was only fifty five years, the style is uniform throughout and for the experts it is the only Catalan, Gothic church which was completely finished during that architectural period. It also has good acoustics encouraging recitals, and the effect of the music in the illuminated church in the evening can be magical.

The square outside the church, the *Plaça Santa Maria*, offers the opportunity of a break in one of several little bars, one of which has the appropriate name of 'La Vinya del Senyor' justifying the claim one can make afterwards of having laboured in the Vineyard of the Lord.

El carrer Montcada

The eastern end of *Santa Maria del Mar* looks on to the *Plaça Montcada* and from there the *carrer Montcada* runs up to the *carrer de la Princesa*. The *carrer Montcada* is a street bordered on both sides by palatial, mediaeval town houses, one of which houses the Picasso Museum and the others either art galleries or other museums. The Picasso Museum is the most visited in the town and almost an obligatory port of call. The artist donated a substantial number of works to the city which had been the jumping-off point of his career, and this collection is the most complete one of his early work although it also includes important examples of his later styles, including his renowned interpretations of Velazquez's *Las Meninas*. The building housing the exhibition is a pleasure to see in itself, a beautifully restored mediaeval town palace. Check the opening times prior to your visit.

The *carrer Montcada* really is a festival of art, door after door leading to museums or art galleries, and a glimpse into the inner courtyards of these ancient town houses will likely induce you inside to see them in all of their splendour.

The port, Maremagnum, the Barceloneta and the Olympic port

Modern Barcelona has been grafted on to the old and nowhere is this better seen than down in the *port vell*, the old port. To see this particular area you can plan it as a walk to finish up with a meal in the *Port Olimpic*. A starting point would be by the statue of Christopher Columbus at the bottom of the Rambla (the *Drassanes* metro station on Line 3). In front of the Columbus statue an undulating wooden walkway, called the *Rambla del Mar* has been built out over the water to an entertainment area on a quay, the *Moll d'Espanya*. This is the *Maremagnum*, a modern pleasure centre with shops, restaurants which include a multi-ethnic, fast food eatery as well as upmarket establishments, bars, a family centre, a vast aquarium specializing in Mediterranean aquatic fish and fauna, an Imax cinema, and so on; the golfer will probably find all this much more fun than being dragged round mediaeval Barcelona. Prior to the Olympics the much-repeated cliché was that Barcelona lived with its back turned to the sea; today, there must be very few major ports in the world where the citizen and visitor can better immerse themselves in the port area than here.

Once you have finished with the *Maremagnum* you walk back to dry land down the landscaped garden area of the *Moll d'Espanya*, which drops you off at the *Palau del Mar*, an attractively redeveloped dockside warehouse which now has restaurants on the ground floor and a museum and offices above. It marks the beginning of the *Barceloneta*, the housing development originally built by a military engineer in the mid-eighteenth century in which the martial fondness for straight lines and orderly deployment give it all the charm of a military barracks. Today, however, it would never pass the Colonel's inspection: exceedingly seedy and with more than its share of delinquency behind the first line of buildings which, unlike those behind, have enviable views out over the redeveloped and spacious *Moll* (quay) *de la Barceloneta*, it is not an area to penetrate except for a visit to one establishment, 'Can Ramonet', a short way down the *carrer de la Maquinista*. This bar/restaurant has a large room set up for the client to eat tapas – the cured ham is excellent – using upturned barrels as tables or if he prefers to eat a meal proper he can move into the restaurant. Either way he will be served excellent quality food and wine, and as a bonus the building itself, built in 1763, is well preserved and the oldest tavern in the port.

When you reach the *Plaça de les Palmeres* after walking along beside the yacht marina you are virtually on the wide *Barceloneta* beach, the town's nearest stretch of sand and a major asset after it was cleaned up and redeveloped. You should now head up the coast towards the Olympic Port, only a few hundred metres away and clearly visible because of the two high rise buildings which back on to it.

The Olympic Port

This was built specially for the '92 Games, right in front of the Olympic village, which itself consists of over two hundred apartments which were sold to the public after the games. It was another successful case of using a major international gathering to sweep away a decayed industrial area, redevelop it and found a new and very desirable residential area. The fortunate buyers look out over the sea and have a park area leading on to a large beach as their back yard. The Olympic port itself is surrounded on two of its sides by restaurants and bars, tens of them, all with outdoor tables supplementing the accommodation inside and the choice of food and prices make it a very attractive rendezvous. The ambience at night in the summer is astonishing, hundreds of people eating out or just wandering around and enjoying the atmosphere. It is a must on your list of Barcelona experiences.

Montjuïc
This is the hill overlooking the port from where General Espartero bombarded the city in 1843. Some of the best views of the town await the visitor to the fort at the top of the hill, today a military museum. Montjuïc was the nerve centre of the Olympic games for which the Olympic Ring, a succession of buildings for different events in the Games, was built. The stadium itself is impressive, the result of remodelling the one built for the 1929 Universal Exhibition but the jewel of them all is the *Palau Sant Jordi*, a vast indoor stadium designed by Arata Isozaki, which stands with its uniquely-domed roof and undulating eaves in a formal stone-paved plaza illuminated at night by tall and elegant beacon lights designed by the architect's wife. Further down the hill is the *Pueblo Español,* also a legacy from the 1929 exhibition and still an interesting corner to walk round and see the architectural styles of buildings from the different Spanish regions. The Miró Foundation not only houses a major collection of the artist's work but is a singularly effective design of a museum building by Josep María Sert. At the bottom of the hill, overlooking the Exhibition grounds and the *Plaça d'Espanya* the *Palau Nacional* housing the *Museo Nacional d'Art de Catalunya* makes a splendid backdrop to the Magic Fountain, with its intricate programme of changing shapes, colours and music, and something to see in the evening if you coincide with one of the few events in the year when the fountain is put through its paces.

El Tibidabo
The 500-metre-high hill behind the town, crowned with a twentieth-century basilica, only merits a visit for the view and the ride up in a restored tram, *el Tramvia Blau,* which departs from the *Plaça John F Kennedy* and shudders and grinds its way up to the bottom end of the funicular railway which takes you dizzily up the last stretch to the top

while giving you an unmatched view over the metropolitan area. Norman Foster's needle-sharp communications tower stands close to the crest looking like a stylish space rocket ready on the launchpad but the basilica is disappointing and the funfair could do the place a big favour by disappearing.

Modern Barcelona

Much of what is new in the city is clever adaptations of old buildings or modernizations of existing institutions, such as the Olympic stadium, so that some of the best of the new is sited in the older parts of the town. But Barcelona is unquestionably the trend-setter in modern Spain, with a reputation for design and for being a place where the latest in style, whether it be clothes, interiors or trendy bars and night spots, forms part of the character of the town. One area where even the buildings are late twentieth century is on the *Diagonal*, the wide avenue which cuts diagonally (hence the name) across the grid of *l'Eixample* beyond the *Plaça Franscesc Macià*. You may find some of the buildings not to your taste but as an example of urban planning, with its wide pedestrian walkways, bicycle paths, trees and space it is a refreshingly broad avenue in a densely built city. If, after strolling up this stretch of the *Diagonal*, a walk in beautiful gardens appeals you can wander round the exterior of the Royal Palace of Pedralbes fronting on to the avenue; the interior is not open to the public.

Inevitably, the latest in international, gimmicky, chain restaurants are all present in the town, from Fashion Café and Planet Hollywood to Hard Rock Café and Dive: you will find them all equally bland unless you go to restaurants to enjoy something other than the food.

Museums

There are forty nine museums listed in the tourist information guide so some selection is obviously necessary if you wish to spend some of your time inside such institutions. The three major art museums are those dedicated to Picasso, Miró and the Thyssen Bornemisa collection in the monastery of Pedralbes, and if modern art is your passion there is a huge offering in different museums and art galleries. The Maritime museum in the mediaeval shipyard of the *Drassanes Reials*, close to La Rambla, is a splendid building in itself, and the *Museu Nacional d'Art de Catalunya* (MNAC) houses the most important collection of Romanesque art in the world, mostly murals extracted from Romanesque churches from all over Catalonia using a special technique to remove the mural paintings and resite them in full scale models inside the museum so that you view them exactly as they were in the original church. While visiting the *Sagrada Família* you can see the museum in the crypt with its display of models of the church and other Gaudí memorabilia. Amazingly, the second most visited museum in the city is the one dedicated to the Barcelona football club which receives over 800,000 visitors per year.

Restaurants

This is the city of a thousand bars and restaurants, every street corner seemingly the site for refreshment of one sort or another. If you enjoy tapas there are several new establishments offering a large selection on *Passeig de Gracia*, which is as pleasant an avenue to stroll along as there is. If asked to name a few of the classic restaurants in town most people would probably include 'Los Caracoles', just off La Rambla on *carrer dels Escudellers*, good value for money and lots of atmosphere but popular with tourists, 'Siete Puertas', one of Barcelona's oldest establishments close to the water on *Passeig Isabel II*, 'Agut d'Avignon' on *carrer Trinitat*, just off *Aviñó*, which in turn leads off the *carrer Ferrán*, a thoroughly Catalan restaurant with some unusual dishes, and 'Senyor Parellada', run by the family who run the 'Fonda de Europa' in Granollers. An up-market restaurant close to *Passeig de Gracia* and an example of elegant modern interior design is 'Tragaluz' on *Passeig Concepció*, where the food matches the surroundings. The Port Olimpic offers a huge choice of restaurants in one small area with the attraction of being able to eat in the open air. Finally, a choice little place for anything from a coffee to a meal is the historic establishment of the '4 Gats', which played frequent host to Picasso and other artists at the turn of the century, and is located on the ground floor of *Casa Marti* a Moderniste building by Puig i Cadalfalch on the *carrer Montsió*, just off *El Portal de l'Angel*. '*Quatre gats*' (four cats), you will remember, is a colloquialism in Catalan meaning just a few people. It was reopened a few years ago and today offers an excellent menu at lunchtime for Ptas 1,500 in surroundings that must be very similar to those in the original café. It even prints a daily broadsheet as did the original establishment.

IV

The Montseny Mountain

Club de Golf Osona – Montanya

If you are a lover of mountain scenery and the feeling of isolation from the modern world which goes with it, then this is your opportunity to indulge, just fifty kilometres from Barcelona and only twenty five from the coast as the crow flies. The Montseny massif is all of 1,712 metres at its highest point, the Turó de l'Home, and the Osona-Montanya-El Brull golf club, to give it its full name, lies at about the 750-metre level on an ample plateau area so one does not have the feeling of playing golf on the side of a mountain. Before a recently built new course in the Vall d'Aran was finished, only the two courses in the district of La Cerdanya in the Pyrenees are higher than Montanya, which, by the way, is the name everyone uses to identify the course.

The easiest way to Montanya is to make for the village of Aiguafreda on the N-152 road, which runs from the outskirts of Barcelona to Ripoll at the foot of the Pyrenees. Aiguafreda is roughly half way between the towns of Granollers and Vic, and once you have passed through the village itself the route up the mountain to the golf course is signposted.

Before leaving your hero to the fate awaiting him on this 6,056 metres (6,667 yard), par seventy two and pleasantly varied course, a coffee or snack at the bar in the clubhouse will give you a chance to visit this imposing stone-built fortress of a building which stands like a sentinel over the course unfolding below it. The first and tenth tees just below the clubhouse both look out over a lake, which on both holes has to be driven to reach the nearest point of the fairway. It is one of the most testing opening tee-shots I know for the higher-handicap golfer, who at this stage of his day does not yet know which particular golf demons are going to play havoc with his swing, and requires a carry of about 160 yards on the first hole, aided by a well elevated tee, and nearer 170 on the tenth. Anyone dumping it into the lake on the first is, naturally, odds-on favourite for an encore on the tenth.

Depending on your mood you might like to witness the master's overture unfold or perhaps be discreet and depart on your day's programme before he transforms into a reluctant Izaak Walton.

Part of the course and the surrounding land were the site for the cross-country equestrian events in the 1992 Olympics and a letter thanking the President and members of the club from Buckingham Palace and signed by a Lady-in-Waiting to the Princess Royal is displayed just by the reception desk, testifying to this byte of sporting history. Between the seventeenth tee and the eighteenth fairway one of the water jumps remains as further evidence of the event.

The scenery around the course is superb, the fairways weaving in and out of woodland, with lakes and streams skirting several holes. and the Montseny mountain rising as a backdrop to the east. Away to the north-west, from the seventh tee and other vantage points, you can see the Pyrenees some seventy kilometres distant and snow-capped from November until late June. In summer although the day temperatures in the sun are high the humidity is much lower than down on the coast, and the evenings and nights are very pleasant. The course remains open throughout the winter but the mountain's microclimate brings a fair amount of rain and the temperatures drop below freezing at night from December until at least the end of February. If you are tempted to stay close to the course the excellent modern Hotel Montanya is only four kilometres down the road. Barcelona Football Club's team stay here and train prior to a big game and several players have summer houses in the area, and that, in Catalonia, means that you will have the privilege of rubbing shoulders with the equivalent of royalty.

The course was opened in 1990 and hosted the 1993 Open de Catalonia, won by Sam Torrance, after being shortened by bad weather. The condition of the course from April to November is usually of a standard that would permit a PGA event to be played there any day of the week. The showers in the changing rooms, by the way, could aptly be called 'acupuncture showers' – they blast high velocity needles of water at you and you are mildly surprised when the torture is over that you are not a bleeding mass of flesh!

The Montseny Natural Park

The course borders on the 35,000 hectares (86,450 acres) of the Montseny Natural Park which has also been declared a Reserve of the Biosphere by Unesco. It has a rich variety of flora and fauna, with several species endemic to the area. You will have little difficulty in finding chestnut trees, ever-green oaks, alders, cork trees, maples and, in the valley of Santa Fé, the southernmost stand of beech trees in the Iberian peninsula. No fir trees in Western Europe, apparently, grow further south than those on the Montseny. Wild boar, woodpigeons, jays, the lynx-like genet, sparrow-hawks, goshawks, chaffinches, the carabus beetle, squirrel rats, and green lizards are not so easy to spot as the trees but are some of the amazingly varied animal life in the park.

The diversity of plants and wildlife results from the different climates prevailing on the mountain. At the lower levels the climate is Mediterranean but above 1,000 metres it is is central-European, with cold winters and sub-humid summers. Some species have mutated to forms unique to the Montseny, such as the Pyrenees triton, the water shrew, and the red frog, and although the insect life in the Park has still not been exhaustively studied species also unique to the area are known to exist.

The Park is a walker's paradise, with signposted walks in different areas. If you decide to explore some of the Park on foot you can buy a detailed map of the area in most of the bookshops in the local towns, and normally the town hall in any village will provide you with free information on the Montseny, usually in Catalan and English, and some do include a map of some of the principal tracks on the mountain. The most complete map is one published by the Natural Parks department of the *Diputación de Barcelona* under the title 'Montseny Parc Natural' which gives exhaustive details of the mountain including most of the tracks.

El Brull

If you feel more like a gentle walk rather than an ambitious trek you could do worse than take off from the golf club for the nearest village of El Brull, heading up the mountain. It's about three kilometres from the clubhouse so you may prefer to take the car and save your legs for the real walks, which start from the village itself.

El Brull is little more than a hamlet but it has a quiet charm, unlike some of the smaller towns and villages in Catalonia which often give the impression that they must be the work of builders and architects who were unrepentantly indifferent to aesthetics. All the buildings around the church and what remains of a castle are built in a garnet-coloured stone, quarried locally. The church of *San Martí de Brull* centres your interest as you approach the village and reveals its age, 1588, by a carving in the lintel over the door while another stone in the belfry records the fact that the bell was cast in Tona in 1791. From a distance, and if the time of day is right, the Moorish-style glazed roof tiles crowning the belfry twinkle like faceted crystals in the sunlight. Right beside the church, with three quite ancient cypresses presiding over it, there is a shop selling local products and across the road is another fine stone building, which is in fact the *Ajuntament*, or town hall. It seems mildly surprising that so small a community should need its own administration centre but in fact the municipality covers quite an extensive area of surrounding land. Somewhat confusingly, there are two dates carved in lintels on the building, 1847 and 1885, which otherwise appears uniform in design and construction. A little way from the centre of the village a few handsome houses stand in well-tended gardens, weekend retreats for a few fortunate families from Barcelona.

There are two restaurants in the village, 'El Castell', close by the ruins of the tenth-century castle, and 'Can Pasqual', adjacent to the *Ajuntament*, so you don't have to starve if your walk leaves you weak with hunger although you may prefer to save your appetite for a more unusual gastronomic experience in Granollers (see page 98).

Just above the *Ajuntament* and restaurant building at the start of a track into the woods stands a signpost giving indications for walks to different farmhouses. The Catalan word *Can* is a contraction of '*ca*', meaning house, and '*en*', which is the article used in Catalan when referring to a person, so '*can*' means 'the house of...' Can Quim translates 'to the house of Quim', and so on. Masia or Mas, which also means a country house or farmhouse in Catalan, is also widely used in Catalonia but on this signpost all destinations are referred to as Can – Can Securum, Can Valls, Can Les planes, etc. You need the 'Parc Natural del Montseny' map to judge the distances of each walk which are not indicated on the signpost, and the map also shows other walks from the village. They are all in beautiful countryside with some memorable views.

For the non-walker there is a road, the BV-5301, which crosses the mountain from the Montanya golf course on the north-west side and heads roughly south-east. It is a good road and although it passes well below the Turó de l'Home you get some fine views of the peak as well as seeing much of the varied terrain and vegetation on the mountain. At the highest point, Coll Formic, you reach the 1,148-metre level before beginning the descent towards the villages scattered down its southern slopes, all of which are worth a visit if you have the time. Here are a some brief comments on a few of them.

The village of Montseny

This is the tiny village from which the mountain gets its name. Most of the houses are built of slate stone in a discreet masia style, each window adorned with a pot of scarlet geraniums in summer giving a dash of colour to the restrained tones of the stone. The church, with its Romanesque bell tower and later architectural styles in the nave and south façade, is built in slate as well. As you quietly observe the ancient stone walls from the sanctuary of the little church garden, each stone a witness to the generations who were baptized, married and received their last rights here, the centuries of history of this tiny community quickly envelop you.

La Costa del Montseny

From the viewing platform in the centre of the village and also from the cemetery you have splendid views over the wide valley of the Vallés Oriental, some five hundred metres below. Behind the diminutive church, so small it looks almost a toy, is the substantial rectory with an enigmatic inscription on a ceramic tile on the wall:

'I without the sun and you without faith are nothing.'

Inside the church you can see a sixteenth-century baptismal font and an alabaster statue of the 'Mother of God of the Angels' from the same period.

Mosqueroles

The church of *St Martí de Mosqueroles* which dates from 1104, when viewed from the north-east is flanked on one side by three pencil-slim cypresses and on the other by an oak. If you are a photographer here is your picture opportunity. Just across the road from the church a track heads off to the west and makes an ideal picnic spot in the shade, looking out over the densely-wooded lower slopes of the Montseny. Sitting here you will hear the church bell chime the hours, just as it has for hundreds of years, the wind in the trees, and perhaps the jingling of bells from grazing cattle, and you won't hear very much else.

By this stage in your day you may be beginning to feel that you have earned your lunch, and you could eat very well by going back to La Costa del Montseny, where the restaurant of the same name specializes in roast kid, and rice with either shell-fish or meat, tomato and diced vegetables sautéed in a casserole, as well as offering a good choice of home-made desserts.

Breda

As an alternative to eating in La Costa del Montseny, you can continue on to Breda, about thirty five kilometres away, which requires driving first to San Celoni and then taking the C-251 until the turn-off for Breda where you have a choice of two interesting restaurants. The first is 'El Montseny', in the centre of the village in what is reputedly its oldest house, Can Trunes, with a history documented back to the fourteenth century. Here you can choose between duck with pears, and canelones and stuffed squid among other dishes of the house.

The other restaurant is 'El Romaní', literally the rosemary herb, which is just outside the village on the road to Arbúcies. In the garden outside the entrance a notice asks guests to refrain from helping themselves to the rosemary growing there because 'it takes a long time to grow'! The decor is tastefully modern and the food is good enough for the restaurant to get a mention in the Michelin Guide for Spain. Entrecôte seasoned with rosemary, petits pois with *botifarra*, which is a very tasty catalan sausage, and pig's trotters cooked with snails are three of their current specialities. If you choose the pig's trotters make sure you flavour them by having a little *all i oli* on your plate; *all i oli* is garlic (*all*) and olive oil (*oli*) pounded into a creamy paste which looks like mayonnaise and has about the same consistency but has a kick that would startle an elephant. It gives a wonderfully vigorous, garlicky tang to all kinds of dishes, and you had better persuade the golfer to eat some too if you're going to share the same car afterwards.

As we are not in a serious Catalan wine growing region you might feel justified in ordering a bottle of a good red wine from another area of

Spain to have with your meal. You could enjoy a bottle of 'Pesquera' from the banks of the Duero, a wine region in central Spain whose fame has recently spread internationally although it is still not as well known as Rioja. Serious Spanish wine connoisseurs maintain that today's finest red wines in the country come from La Ribera del Duero. Among them is 'Vega Sicilia', the most expensive wine in the country, but maybe you should keep that experience for a special occasion, a day when he's shot five under his handicap perhaps. 'Pesquera' is a very good quality red but as the amount produced is limited many restaurants are unable to purchase it for their cellars so don't be surprised if the restaurant of your choice does not include it on their wine list. The agent for 'Pesquera' in Catalonia has to ration his customers each year to ensure that everyone gets at least a sniff of the wine, and it's very difficult to join his list of clients.

Wherever you finally decide to eat you could try a glass of a liqueur called 'Aromas del Montserrat' with ice as an aperitivo or without to round off your meal. It's made under the patronage of Montserrat Abbey, and is as pleasantly aromatic as the name suggests. If you choose to lunch in Breda the 'Bar de la Plaça' is a choice location to have your pre-lunch drink where you can sit outside under the maple trees and observe the gentle routine of village life unfold before you.

Ever since the twelfth century Breda has been under the permanent scrutiny of Montsoriu castle, towering over the village from a vantage point some five hundred metres above on a nicely symmetrical hill four kilometres away. Breda itself is older with the year 878 recorded on its oldest document but the building which catches your attention from every corner of the village is the monastery of *San Salvador*, founded in 1038 by the Viscounts of Girona, Guerau and Ermessenda. Ermessenda sounds melodious enough but you will, arguably, make your best shot at pronouncing the over-dipthongal 'Guerau' with your mouth full of cherries.

What you see today and all that remains of the original Romanesque building is the splendid five-storey bell tower, built in the eleventh century and standing thirty two metres high. The nave of the church is Gothic and was two hundred years under construction between the fourteenth and sixteenth centuries. In the buttress to the apse erosion has hollowed out what must be very soft stone, and today a colony of pigeons nest there, each pigeon in its own stone hollow, looking

like monks in contemplation in their individual niches in a monastic
choir.

A tiny corridor, *el corredor negre*, leads from the back of the church
to the *Pati de l'abadía* – the abbey patio, built in the fifteenth century
and beautifully restored a few years ago. There is a fine covered terrace
on one side and a greengrocer's shop uninhibitedly installed in an
archway on the opposite side. Outside the patio on the north side is what
remains of the abbey cloister, embellished by a tall cypress tree growing
beside it.

Breda is a centre for decorative ceramics and in the centre of the town
adjacent to the Town Hall is the Josep Aragay museum. He was an artist
who lived in Breda and was responsible for introducing ceramics to the
community, and the trade still flourishes today. The building housing the
museum is unusual in that the main part of it is in the transept and apse
of the church of *Santa Maria*, dating from the twelfth century. Recently
someone with iconoclastic leanings built an ugly addition to the
building which sits on the beautiful old church like a horse-fly on an ice
cream.

Before leaving Breda you should stroll to a pleasant little garden
called *La Bassa del Molí*, the Mill Pond, just off the the main square. The
mill stream runs down one side of the garden and from here you have
the best view of Montsoriu castle.

Arbúcies

Once in Breda, a short side-trip to Arbúcies is worthwhile if you have
the time. It is only ten kilometres and you drive through thickly-wooded
countryside past Montsoriu castle, which you can reach on foot by
following a track at the base of the hill and which you will find easily
once you've parked roughly abreast of the castle; it will take you about
half an hour to reach the top.

As you enter Arbúcies you drive past the mineral water bottling plant
of 'Agua Font' opposite which and right beside the road is a natural
spring, where there are usually several cars lined up waiting their turn to
fill large plastic containers with free water – presumably the same as
that sold under the name of 'Agua Font'. Bottled mineral water, a
significant industry on the Montseny, is now sold all over Catalonia and
much of the rest of Spain. The other main bottling plant is in St Hilari de
Sacalm where water sold under the brand name of 'Font Vella' is

produced. Both are 'still' waters, and there are few households which do not rely on bottled water for drinking. The water in Barcelona can be so strongly chlorinated that it is virtually undrinkable, and it makes tea and coffee taste like something only a Martian would drink.

There is an excellent carbonated mineral water bottled outside the Montseny massif but quite close to it at Caldas de Malavella, where the source of 'Vichy Catalan' is located and has provided drinking water ever since Roman times. The water emerges at a temperature of sixty degrees centigrade and 'Vichy Catalan' is similar to the French Vichy water in taste and in the abundance of minerals naturally present in the water; it can be a real bonus in aiding an over-taxed stomach digest a meal and is also recommended for the liver and arthritis.

Caldas de Malavella is also a thriving spa with thousands of patients benefiting from the therapeutic qualities of its waters every year. If your golfer is beginning to complain of back problems as a result of his Catalan tour there are a number of excellent spas in the region where you could lay him up while you pursue your carefully chosen programme. If you do, more likely than not after two days of drinking only mineral water and being bathed and battered into muscular condition by some robust Catalan matron, who tend to have the strength, weight and sheer mass of an ox, he'll tell you that he's in fine shape to continue with his golf and probably won't mention his back again in years.

What makes a visit to Arbúcies worthwhile is the *Gabella* Ethnological Museum of the Montseny where a remarkable display of artifacts, models, tableaux and real-life products traces the history of man on the mountain from prehistoric settlements to modern times. There is, for example, an excellent topographical model of the area round Arbúcies showing the exact location of 272 masias, each identified by name and classified by historical period. As you would expect in a museum of human activity from prehistoric times to the present day, there are details to surprise you such as the design of buttons used in the fourteenth century, which is practically the same as those of today, or that, prior to the industrialization of ice-making, one of the commercial activities in Arbúcies was to cut ice from the frozen lakes on the upper levels of the mountain, then store it in 'ice wells' which kept the ice below freezing point, prior to transporting it to customers in Barcelona. With cork trees growing abundantly on the mountain, making a well insulated, thermal container to transport the ice would not have been difficult but even so the time taken by a horse-drawn cart from Arbúcies to the city would have been considerable; perhaps it was taken overnight.

Once industrialization began to take hold in the town two industries developed naturally from previously existing trades: specialist coach-building followed on from cart- and carriage-making, and the lathe-working of wood was a natural derivative of carpentry. The manufacture of textiles also developed in parallel with the coach-building to meet the demand of the upholsterers. You can also see comprehensive displays of tools and artifacts used in farming, basket-making, ironworking, hunting and the making of *alpargatas* – rope-soled sandals – which were the traditional footwear in rural Catalonia and are still worn today by some people during the summer months. The museum also has an information centre on the Montseny Natural Park, a library, and houses the historic archives of town. The opening times for the museum are 11 a.m. to 2 p.m., and 5 p.m. to 8 p.m. from Tuesdays to Saturdays, and 11 a.m. to 2 p.m. on Sundays; it is closed on Mondays.

Arbúcies is at the foot of the north side of the mountain and is surrounded by thick woodlands. Josep Pla in his *Guia de Catalunya* describes it as 'the garden city of the Montseny' but while the town does have two pleasant parks, you can't avoid thinking that Pla must have had very enjoyable personal memories of the place, perhaps a girlfriend or two, to award it such a flattering description.

If after your visit to the *Gabella* museum your feet need a rest the *Plaça de la Vila* is short distance down the *carrer Major*, just past the *Ajuntament*, and is as nice a setting for a restorative drink as you will find in the central part of the town. There is a centenarian plane tree planted in the middle of the gently-sloping square with a low circular stone bench round its base, and in the upper corner of the square you can sit outside the bar 'La Plaça' (yes, that name again! Bar owners in this corner of the world must want to make sure that even a golfer can remember the name of their bar) and perhaps pass the time trying to think up a more seductive adjective than polygonal to describe the shape of the plaça. Really, though, at two in the afternoon on a sunny June day, it is a pleasant, unpretentious, homely sort of square with a columned walkway round two sides and the walls of the surrounding buildings freshly painted in pastel shades of brown, ochre and rose, marred only by the cables festooned along the walls at eaves level as so often is the case in Spain. The *carrer Major* and the *Plaça* are a pedestrian precinct with almost no traffic allowed through.

El Turó de l'Home

In case you are naturally inclined to mountaineering and can never resist the temptation to scale any peak which happens to be within striking distance, (if so, why do you have a golfer in tow rather than a mountaineer?) here are the alternative routes you can take on foot and by car to get you to the Turó de l'Home peak. By car, you would take the same road, the BV-5301, from Montanya Golf Club through El Brull and over Coll Formic; after passing the village of Montseny turn off for La Costa del Montseny. Continue on after passing this village for about another ten kilometres until you reach a road off to your left which takes you up the final stretch, almost to the peak itself. If the day is clear the views on all sides will not disappoint you. The Costa Brava is relatively close and you can see a long way up it but people say that in exceptionally clear conditions it's even possible to see Mallorca, some two hundred kilometres away. To reach El Turó de l'Home on foot you have two strategic options: either choose your starting point somewhere on the BV-5301 or from a point on the BV-5114, which runs from Sant Celoni to Santa Fe. Again, you will need your map of the Parc Natural del Montseny to pick out which track you are going to follow.

A meal in La Fonda Europa in Granollers

For most people a meal in genuine period surroundings adds another dimension to the pleasure of eating out. 'La Fonda de Europa' in Granollers, some twenty seven kilometres to the north of Barcelona, is such a place, where the 1930s atmosphere has, happily, never been allowed to disappear.

The 'Fonda', the word translates as 'inn', is about as central as you can get in Granollers, fronting on to the *Anselmo Clavé* mainstreet and just off the *Plaça de la Porxada* with its handsome covered market-place. Although 1858 is carved over the main entrance the hotel dates back to 1714 and has undergone several restorations in the intervening years, the last one in preparation for the 1992 Olympics when the previously spartan first-floor bedrooms were completely rebuilt and today are up to international standards. There are only seven bedrooms available until the two remaining floors are eventually refurbished so you have to book well ahead if you choose to stay here. The current price of a room for two people is Ptas 10,000 a night. The stylistically flowery façade at the back of the hotel, designed by Josep Maria Miró and embellishing one corner of the otherwise dreary *Plaça de Berangé*, was an improvement added in 1923.

The 'Fonda' has been in the Parellada family for two hundred years and is currently managed by Ramón Parellada, the sixth generation to do so. He claims that their family is probably the oldest in the catering business in Catalonia simply because in the past most people in the business, if successful, ensured that their children were educated for one of the professions, and if the business failed it closed. The Parelladas also own and manage a well known restaurant in Barcelona, 'El Senyor Parellada', currently considered pretty high up the league in value for money given the quality of the food served, and also have an interest in the new 'Ciutat de Granollers' hotel, also in Granollers.

Such has been the reputation of the 'Fonda' over the past 150 years that the list of famous personalities to have patronized the place must be unrivalled by any other establishment in Catalonia outside Barcelona. From royalty, Alfonso XIII, to artists, including Picasso, Dalí, Rusinyol and Tapiès, and from presidents of government to writers such as Cela, Pla, Verdaguer and Maragall, all have come here and eaten and chatted under the Fonda's roof. Ramón Parellada, whose artist wife designed the menu cover, hopes that one or more of his children will follow him into the business and continue the family tradition; it would be a sad loss if none of them did because only personal commitment can maintain the character of such a place.

The 'Fonda Europa' has always been the meeting point for the locals, who use the bar and cafeteria area at all hours of the day and night to meet friends or just to down a quick coffee or a brandy while chatting to the ever amiable barman. On Thursdays, which is market day in Granollers and has been ever since the town was founded in 944 with occasional breaks when political commotion temporarily interrupted civil routines, the 'Fonda' is packed with people from seven in the morning until about noon, all eating the Catalan equivalent of brunch, *esmorçar amb forquilla* – a morning snack which requires a fork. At every table groups of men, occasionally accompanied by a wife, are eating anything from beans with pork sausage to salt cod with onions and olives, or a plate of assorted cold meats, all washed down with a local wine. If this sounds a bit too much for you to digest at this hour of the day while you observe the scene, you might order a coffee with 'Diplomatics', which turn out to be tasty little pastries.

Over the tables noisy deals are done between farmers and tradespeople, gossip is exchanged and secrets confided. The 'Fonda' as with 'Fonda's' in other country towns in Catalunya, becomes for this one morning of the week the trading floor for agricultural deals just as though it was the official Exchange. It makes a vivid tableau of a rural community going about its business while mingling with friends and acquaintances.

The bar itself is in fact a sort of foyer to the restaurant, separated from it by red velvet curtains, and the two are decorated in the same style. The lights are what you might call 'nineteen-forties-sitting-room-lamp-shades' with low wattage bulbs, arranged in banks to give a muted diffused lighting effect somewhat reminiscent of the drowsy lighting in blacked-out homes in the Second World War. In the restaurant the ceiling is the standard Catalan beam construction with the beams painted dark brown, looking almost black in the subdued light at night. The rows of tables in the main area are partially separated from each other by the high-backed bench seats behind each table, hinting at rather than providing a suggestion of privacy for your patch in the restaurant. There are large allegorical paintings on the walls which hasn't discouraged the management from placing a coathanger stand bang in front of one of them. The tables are small, too small to hold side-plates as well as the main dish so you eat your bread off the table as is customary in most dining rooms in Catalonia, and are covered with blue-bordered white cotton table-cloths; the glassware was clearly chosen for endurance rather than elegance and the cutlery is standard caterers'. Overall, the style is simple, clean, and small-town sensible.

The à la carte menu is however anything but simple and is uncompromisingly Catalan, and the cooking is well up to the extensive choice on offer. There are over seventy dishes listed including the salads and excluding the desserts, and every one can be recommended. The *esqueixada de bacallà* – cold salt cod with tomatoes, onions and oil, *ànec amb figues* – duck cooked with figs, or *calamarcets de costa a la planxa amb all i julivert* – baby squid cooked on the grill with garlic and parsley, are just three you might try. The Head Waiter will usually tell you what special dishes are recommended for the day based on whatever was a good buy in the market that morning but everything on the menu can be ordered with confidence. The portions are man-sized, the ingredients are always fresh and the cooking is deservedly a by-word in the area.

Depending on what you choose for your meal you might try a Torres Coronas red wine to accompany it. The grapes in this wine are 86% Tempranillo and 14% Cabernet Sauvignon and the result is a pleasant full-bodied Claret, matured for fifteen months in American oak. Alternatively if you prefer a white wine you could order a Viña Sol, also produced by Torres, one of the leading Catalan wineries in the Penedès area south of Barcelona who pioneered back in the early sixties the introduction of Catalan wines into the rest of Europe.

The service in the restaurant matches the quality of the food and the surroundings. The waiters are true professionals, trained in the art, immaculately groomed and attired in short waist-length black jackets with black bow-tie and white shirt. From the waist down a wrap-around white apron reaches down to their shoes and a standard-issue waiter's white napkin hangs at the ready over the left arm. Reserved and unfussed they quietly and efficiently cater to your needs, but do not expect much English. No summer vacation jobs for students here – you'd need at least a waiter's diploma to qualify for the first interview.

If you decide to dine at the 'Fonda' on Friday or Saturday evening you should reserve a table by phone, on 93-8700312, because the place will be packed. At lunchtime you can drop in on the whim of the moment and you should be able to get a table somewhere in the three areas that restaurant comprises. On Thursday mornings just breeze in and join the market melée!

The 'Fonda' is no more than a two minute walk from the *Plaça de la Porxada* where all that's worth seeing in this 50,000-population town is located. Stroll down the *carrer Esperança*, a pleasant narrow pedestrian street almost opposite the entrance to the hotel and you will immediately see the *Porxada*, a splendid pillared construction open on all four sides but roofing over the area below. Originally built as a granary in 1587 it has undergone several renovations, the dates of which are carved on the wooden beams under the roof. The last such was in 1986 and the result is a magnificent wooden structure in perfect condition supporting a tiled roof and resting on three rows of Doric stone columns. The *Porxada* provides a covered area on market days where vendors set out their stalls and on other days any other outdoor event taking place is usually located there unless a larger space is needed.

On the west side of the *plaça* close to the *Porxada* is the town hall with its stylish Moderniste Neo-Gothic façade. What you see today was designed by the architect Simó Cordomí i Carrera who remodelled the building between 1902 and 1904. The original building on the site was mediaeval but had been frequently altered down the centuries. Seen as you enter the *plaça* from the *carrer Esperança* it contrasts nicely with the *Porxada*. Behind the the *Plaça de la Porxada* and clearly visible from it is the bell tower of the church of *Sant Esteve* built in the fifteenth century and all that remains of the original Gothic church.

The 'Fonda de Europa' is within thirty minutes drive by car from several golf courses: Sant Cugat, Vallromanes, Montanya, Can Bosch, Caldas International Golf Club and Llavaneres.

Sant Miquel del Fai

Only twenty five kilometres from the town of Granollers lies one of those topographical features of such impressive proportions that it could probably be included in your list of memorable natural sights you have seen in your life. This one is a 350-metre-deep limestone gorge, one side of which is practically vertical.

To reach the gorge you have to drive to St Feliu de Codines, which you can reach by taking the N-152 from just outside Granollers to L'Ametlla del Vallés and then follow the road to Bigas before continuing on to St Feliu de Codines. From here the route to Sant Miquel del Fai is well signposted.

Some people have a fear of heights and the road from St Feliu de Codines to the gorge may be a severe test of your nerve in this respect. You reach one side of the gorge almost as soon as you leave St Feliu, and from there on the road is cut high into the side of the gorge with an almost vertical drop of about three hundred metres to your right. If your nerves permit you to look, the views are memorable all the way although if you're driving you will need to keep your eye on the road in case you meet a bus on a bend coming the other way!

Male sufferers from the horror-of-heights syndrome have varying reactions to the moments of numbing terror that can almost paralyze you when you're exposed to some hideous dropping-away of solid earth right before your feet. The English expressions of 'heart in mouth', 'sweaty palms' and 'white about the gills' or plain 'chicken' get nowhere near the outright panic some can feel. Spaniards, never shy at using a choice expletive to add a little emphasis, get closer with having your 'balls in your throat' or more simply '*acojonado*' which translates roughly as 'balls-ed up', meaning one supposes that they have more or less 'retracted', so temporarily – you hope – you've effectively been neutered. Again, some feel the equivalent of a dull toothache but it's located, as you may have guessed, in that binary peripheral to the CPU, to use the jolly language only found in computer manuals. Anyway, you now know what a pain in the binaries is. Women have no such childish fears and will quite happily strut about on the very edge of an abyss as though no one had ever disappeared forever through such foolhardy behaviour. If your man with the harmonious swing is with you on this excursion and is one of the tribe inclined to get tingly feet at the very least when faced with a bottomless chasm you might suggest that he sits in the back of the car and takes a ten-minute nap, which is about the time you will need to reach the head of the gorge from St Felíu de Codines. Once there the worst is over; except, of course, you still have to return to St Felíu!

At the head of the gorge and about half way up the rock face is what remains of the monastery of *Sant Miquel* which today consists of the Priory building. You have to pay an entry fee to gain access to the priory and surrounding area but it is worth the price. You can park the car in an open space which is just behind the head of the gorge, and from there you walk down through a narrow cleft in a rock and emerge onto the path which runs round the gorge face to the priory building and church. The spectacle of the narrow valley of Riells at the bottom of the gorge stretching away in front of you, the head of the gorge falling vertically below your feet and to your right a waterfall fed by the river Tenes cascading down from above the gorge, is impressive. The path continues on past the priory and actually passes behind the waterfall and on to the little Romanesque church of *Sant Martí* which stands on a small terrace of land jutting out from the west side of the gorge some eight hundred metres further on.

The priory building is early fifteenth-century Gothic and is believed to have been built by Luis de Castellbell i de Cordelles, who was Prior from

1398 to 1427. The building is considered to be one of the finest examples of Gothic architecture in Catalonia and has been preserved in its original form to the present day.

Today it houses a restaurant and bar, both with prime views out over the valley of Riells below. You can also visit the first floor which was the original refectory where you can see paintings of St George, patron saint of Catalonia, and of the martyrdom of Santa Eulalia of Barcelona.

Immediately adjacent to the priory building is a large man-made pond which supplied water to the priory and which is fed by the waters of the river Rossinyol. This little river, usually not much more than a stream, flows down from above the gorge into the pond and exits again down over the the rock edge into the valley below. From this side of the priory you will see various small annexes which have been built over the years and which inevitably detract from the clean lines of the original building.

The monastery was founded between 997 and 1006 but little is known about the original monastic building although documents do reveal that the community never had more than ten members. The church of *St Miquel del Fai*, about which more later, was consecrated in 1006. The first abbot was Willemundus and originally the monastery was an independent institution but less than fifty years later it was made a dependency of the monastery of St Victor of Marseilles together with several other Catalan monasteries, and henceforth it became a priory.

Monks continued to live in the Priory until 1525 when Fray Andrés de Arbizu, the last resident monk, died. In 1567 the pope made *St Miquel del Fai* a secular church to be administered by the Archdeacons of Girona Cathedral, one of whom was responsible for constructing the small Rossinyol bridge built in 1592 over which you walk today to enter the head of the gorge. There were never less than two priests living in the monastery over the years until 1835, after which the Parish priest of Riells celebrated mass in the church on most Sundays and on the two feast days of St Miquel. Sadly, in 1936 the church was badly damaged through anti-clerical vandalism in the early stages of the Spanish Civil War and religious services ceased until its recent restoration.

The 'Fai' part of the name of St Miquel del Fai is a derivative of the word Fall, with the same meaning as the English word as in the 'Niagara Falls'. The word 'fall' was in use centuries ago in Catalonia but subsequently evolved to 'Fai' because the double 'l' in the eastern part of Catalonia is pronounced as 'ai'.

The church of *Sant Miquel del Fai* is in fact a cave in the wall of rock soaring up behind the priory building and is the largest and best preserved church of this type in Spain. The ceiling and part of the floor is natural rock although the ceiling in the chancel has Gothic pointed arches spanning the underside of the rock and is believed to have been an attempt to extend the church in the fifteenth century. The earliest document referring to it is dated 997 in which Count Ramón Borrell gave it to a nobleman, Gombau de Besora, for him to found a monastery there.

The whole area round the priory and church is full of caves, some of which can be visited, and everywhere you walk water seeps out of the rock wall creating rivulets which nourish the mosses and aquatic plants growing on the rock. What was abundant vegetation on the sides and terraces of the gorge was ravaged two years ago by that plague of the Catalan summer, a forest fire, but as the natural Mediterranean vegetation soon reestablishes itself the sides of the valley will regain their former look within a few years.

The church of *St Martí* which you can see from the priory and can be reached by following the path which runs behind the waterfall, is the oldest centre of religious worship in the district with a history documented back to 878, more than a hundred years older than the church of *St Miquel.* What you see today is a Romanesque reconstruction of the original church carried out in the thirteenth century. The church is in a poor state of maintenance and its two important mediaeval mural paintings have been taken to the permanent exhibition of Romanesque art in Barcelona to ensure their preservation.

A place in such a dramatic setting and with centuries of history behind it has, naturally, its share of legends. One tells of how the Archangel St Michael (Sant Miquel) cleared the caves of pagan worshippers of the goddess Venus and swept the evil fairies into the depths of the whirlpools and eddies of the river in the valley below. Thereafter on moonlit nights they sing enticingly to strangers who, if they are unwise enough to ask whose voices can be heard from the depths of the water, are told that they are the fairies of the valley who have fallen into the river and plead for help. If the stranger attempts to save them he is drawn down into the water, never to emerge again.

Another legend tells of a convent which had been built on the rock face where the remains of a wooden beam jutting out from the rock and part of a staircase cut into the rock could be seen. A thousand years or more ago on the night of a terrible storm the building was sent hurtling into the valley by a stroke of lightning while the nuns were indulging in a thoroughly unholy orgy. Those at the back of the class who have already jumped to the conclusion that it must have been the neighbouring monks who were carousing with them on this black night are, as usual, wrong. The legend says that handsome young gentlemen from the valley had come up to the convent, attracted by the famed beauty of the nuns.

V

Girona

Golf Girona

Perched high above the town of Girona and just a couple of kilometres on the Girona North exit of the A-17, down the C-150 road to Banyoles and Olot lies this testing course cut out of dense woodland. At 6,058 metres (6,625 yards) from the yellow tees it is anything but short and many of the holes play longer than their yardage because they climb all the way from tee to green. Water, mercifully, only really comes into play on four holes but the trees with thick undergrowth lining most of the fairways place a premium on direction over length in the overall strategy.

From the clubhouse there is a glorious panorama looking west over the woods with the Rocacorba Sierra, 985 metres at its highest point, forming the horizon to the north-west and to the south-west the Montseny mountain rises almost twice as high some forty kilometres away. All you see are trees with an occasional church spire breaking through to give you some perspective. This kind of woodland is what you find all over the interior of the province of Girona up to the higher slopes of the Pyrenees and largely consists of various species of pine, oaks, evergreen oaks, and cork trees although beech, chestnut, willows, and eucalyptus, among others, can be found depending on the soil and the presence of water.

The course is a severe test of stamina for the golfer who chooses to walk it so it might be a good idea for him to tuck in to a plate of cured ham or a substantial *bocadillo* before he starts his round. In the summer months it's advisable to take plenty of drinking water and to hire a golf buggy: the prospect of the continuous climb up from the fourteenth tee all the way to the eighteenth tee is one that would make even a Sherpa blanch.

The tee-shot on the par five first hole sets the parameters for the rest of the round. With a lake to the left and two awkwardly placed pine trees encroaching on the right, hitting the ball through to the safety of the fairway is about as easy as threading a needle in the dark; it is inhibitingly narrow for the shorter hitter who cannot confidently drill it straight over those two pines or who cannot produce a controlled fade at will. The second tee offers an equally tight perspective although the restrictions here are trees left and right but once through the narrow part of the fairway you are left with a frank shot to the green, and this is the case on almost all of the holes on the course. Generally, the greens are well bunkered and can be rather slow.

As you play your way round this very pretty course there are some glorious views away over the woods and every two or three holes an old stone-built masia appears with the entrance facing south, de rigueur in the Catalan countryside, and just a hundred or so metres to the right of the sixteenth tee stands what is left of a fortified mediaeval tower. You are in deep woodland and the only sounds to be heard are the birds, the wind in the trees and the occasional lament of the errant golfer, probably '*Collóns!*' (those binaries again) if he's a local.

With his concentration back on the course the ninth tee will once again remind the visitor of the virtue of keeping to the straight and narrow and although this is a par five of 469 metres (513 yards) it plays sharply downhill after the first shot so he can sacrifice length for accuracy, play an iron off the tee and still have only a short iron in the green for the third shot. The fourteenth is the stroke index 1 hole on this course, playing uphill for 411 metres (449 yards) and dog-legging to the right with the green hidden behind the pines lining the jungle running all the way from tee to green on the right. The par three fifteenth is the only hole on the back nine where water really comes into play and it requires a good tee-shot to clear it; out-of-bounds lurks to the right. As if to console you after the exertions of climbing up the last four holes the par five eighteenth is downhill from tee to green and is the best birdie opportunity on the course, provided the tee-shot is hit to the right-hand side of the left-sloping fairway to avoid it sliding down into the rough and, often, out-of-bounds.

When he finally returns to the clubhouse there will be few times that the golfer will ever feel he has earned his after-round drink more than at Golf Girona. If he has played to his handicap he could take a siesta – he'll be ready for it – in preparation for a major celebration in the evening.

El vall d'en Bas (The valley of En Bas) and Vic

While the golfer wears himself out on Golf Girona's course, which he will if he walks it, you can spend a relaxing and very scenic day in the heartland of Girona province. This is a round trip which has splendid vistas, charming villages and rewarding buildings to see and interesting food to be eaten, all located in the districts of La Garrotxa and Osona.

The Vall d'en Bas is a small valley lying just a few kilometres before you reach the town of Olot, some forty eight kilometres from Girona. To get there take the N-141 road out of Girona to Anglés, and from there on towards Amer and Olot. Four kilometres after Anglés, just after passing through the village of La Cellera de Ter, you cross over the river Ter just below the last sluice-gates of the vast Sau-Susqueda reservoir. This huge man-made complex of water is over twenty four kilometres long with a system of damns built in strategic narrows along the course of the river Ter, and from here Barcelona and a large number of the towns and villages all the way to the coast get their water. There is a small slip-road you can take after crossing the bridge which goes up past the sluice and if you want to get a view of the last stretch of the reservoir you can make a short sortie up it; however later in the day there will be better vantage points for viewing the upper reaches of the reservoir.

As you drive on towards the Vall d'en Bas through a fertile valley scattered with plantations of poplar trees, all laid out in precise symmetric patterns and destined for the paper industry, you get ever deeper into unspoilt countryside, your breadth of view limited by the Sierra del Puig del Moro to your left and the Sierra de las Medas to the right, both densely wooded. You are now in the district of La Garrotxa, an area with a diversity of just about everything – mountains, trees, crops, rivers and landscapes. You finally emerge into the Vall d'en Bas when you descend to the village of Sant Esteve d'en Bas, which is a good point to start your acquaintanceship with the ancient little villages dotted around the valley.

St Esteve d'en Bas

On a weekday the sensation of time having frozen a century or two ago pervades the clean tidy streets of this village which twist and turn around, and even duck under, 300-year-old buildings, most of them built in stone. Like all the villages in the Vall, St Esteve should be wandered round slowly letting the mood of the place seep into your pores, and you need follow no predetermined route because you can cover all of the old part with your instinct acting as guide in less than twenty minutes. The church and adjacent square are a good starting point, and every so often you turn a corner and there is a handsome view out over the Vall d'en Bas with some of its eight villages laid out in front of you.

When you leave Sant Esteve take the road to Olot, the capital of the district of La Garrotxa and the starting point for possible visits to the volcanic craters formed some 11,500 years ago making the area into what is considered the best example of a volcanic region in the Iberian Peninsula and which was declared a Natural Park by the Catalan parliament in 1982.

Probably the prettiest crater is just outside the mediaeval village of Santa Pau, about nine kilometres from Olot, from where, if you prefer to, you can walk along a well signposted route up to the top of the perfectly conical crater of Santa Margarida to find to your delight that down inside is a meadow with a tiny church, or hermitage as they are referred to locally, dedicated to *Santa Margarida*, planted right in the centre of the 300-metre-diameter rim. The walk will take you something over an hour and a half there and back. These craters are covered in vegetation, the porous volcanic subsoil, which retains humidity, contributing to the richness of the plant life in the area. Beech woods are common too, one of which, *La Fageda* (beech wood) *d'en Jordá*, was the inspiration for one of Joan Maragall's poems with its opening line 'Do you know where the *fageda d'en Jordá* is?' Well, now you do but who was *en Jordá*?

The town of Olot has one artistic treasure, the painting by El Greco of 'Christ on the cross' which you might consider deserves a visit; it is normally kept in the museum of the church of *St Esteve* but is frequently lent to other museums and galleries for exhibitions so it is advisable to confirm its availability for viewing by phone with the Rectory on (972) 690225. The town has produced several noteworthy landscape painters over the last hundred years known collectively as the 'Olot School', including the Veyredas, Berga, Boix, Marsillach and still painting today, Josep Colomer and his son, Josep Colomer Valls. Josep Clarà, one of the most respected Catalan twentieth-century sculptors, also lived here and the town has assembled a fine collection of his work from all over Catalonia. All these can be viewed in the *Museu Comarcal de la Garrotxa* on *l'Hospici d'Olot* street.

The villages of El Mallol, St Privat d'en Bas and Hostalets d'en Bas

Back in the Vall d'en Bas, there are at least three other little villages worth a quick visit. El Mallol is less than two kilometres down the road from Les Preses to Sant Privat d'en Bas, and is another splendid example of stone-built balconied houses fronting on to narrow stone-paved streets. The ancestral home of the Viscounts of Bas, right in the heart of the village, has been nicely restored and crowning everything is the eighteenth-century church of *St Bartolomeu*.

St Privat d'en Bas is another three kilometres on from el Mallol and after an uninteresting first impression as you enter the village you eventually come to the tiny square just below the church, rather plain and simple and rustic. What you most notice is the sense of almost complete isolation of the place, tucked up under the rising ground behind, the essence of rural life. St Privat, in case you were wondering, was a soldier and martyr who was flogged to death in 222 on orders of the emperor Alexander.

The Vall d'en Bas is renowned for its *charcuterie* and this village produces some varieties of cured pork sausage which are very good. Ask for *Llom* and choose a large diameter version; sliced thin and eaten on *pan con tomate – pa amb tomaquet* in Catalan – or by itself with a glass of fino, it makes an appetizing tapa.

Once back on the main road from Olot to Vic a quick side trip to Els Hostalets d'en Bas rewards you with a village of handsome, three-storeyed stone houses running as a terraced street towards the church. What distinguishes it from the other villages are the continuous wooden balconies running at the first and second floor levels with the overhanging roof adding protection from the rain. In the summer months the geraniums in flower pots make these balconies a riot of colour. The church of the *Assumption* is appealing from the outside but disappointing within, the victim of an unimaginative renovation. Lintels on some of the houses in the village date their construction early in the eighteenth century, one such reciting 'Gaspar Sola made me in 1727'. At the entrance to the village there is a bakery proudly proclaiming its wood-fired oven and where you can buy one or two-kilo loaves of bread which you may find require more than the usual dosing of oil and tomato to lighten the passage of a what is a pretty solid example of the daily staple, wood-fired oven not withstanding.

You might prefer to eat in the Vall d'en Bas area rather than wait until you reach Vic. If so there are two restaurants in both Els Hostalets d'en Bas and Santa Pau, and of course more in Olot. The beans grown around Santa Pau, known locally as *fesols*, are famed for their quality, derived, it seems, from the volcanic subsoil. Until fairly recently beans were a basic component of a family's diet all over Catalonia and a cauldron of them would be hanging permanently over the fire in the masias, ready at all times of the day for whoever came in hungry from the fields; they are eaten with a generous sprinkling of olive oil after several hours over a low flame in water with some diced potatoes and salt added. You could be excused for thinking that eating them thus is a case of over-zealous compliance with an authentic peasant recipe but they are surprisingly tasty as described. Fortunately for you, if you're not convinced, most of the restaurants in the area do prepare them with the local sausage (*botifarra*), which certainly adds to their appeal, and *botifarra amb mongetes* (sausage with beans) is still a basic dish everywhere in Catalonia and should be tried at least once. A stew of wild boar (*estofat de porc senglar*), oxtail cooked with sepia (*cua de bou amb sèpia*) and veal with a sauce of wild mushrooms (*vedella amb bolets*) are just a few of the dishes on the local menus.

This is an opportunity to try one of the Rosé wines from the Ampurdan – Costa Brava D.O., known for their intense colour and body, the product of the generally sandy porous soil in the area and a generous number of sunlight hours per year as well as sharp contrasts in temperature and fairly abundant rainfall. These Rosé wines are light, fresh and full of flavour, and a chilled bottle of Vinya Orlina would be nicely representative of the type.

The trip from the Vall d'en Bas to Vic is about fifty kilometres of very scenic driving over Collsacabra, the sierra separating Vic from Olot, which starts with a climb of 900 metres in the space of three and a half kilometres, all of it through woodland until you reach the Coll de Condreu at the 1,010-metre level. There are some grand views away towards the south-east and an occasional glimpse of the Sau Susqueda reservoir below. As you round a corner a little hermitage sitting in a copse of trees in a meadow and with no other buildings in sight will likely come into view; isolated hermitages have been sprinkled around generously over this part of Catalonia. At Can Bach you pass close to a magnificent escarpment, rearing up seemingly from nowhere, a mass of ochre-coloured rock.

As you begin to drop down towards Vic, there are roads off to Rupit, a famously pretty village and a favourite subject for painters, and to Cantonigròs. You also pass close by the village of L'Esquirol, also known as Santa María de Corcò, which gave its name inadvertently to the term used all over Spain for someone who crosses a picket line while a strike is on, what in Britain is referred to as a scab. Early this century a factory owner in Manlleu had a strike on his hands and brought in substitute workers from the nearby village of L'Esquirol, and the name has stuck; unfortunate for the village but a decided improvement on the English term!

Vic

The capital of the district of Osona, Vic, is an ancient and prosperous town lying in the plain of the same name and as you drive towards it through lush fields and meadows it's not altogether surprising to learn that the two traditional industries in the town are cured meats and leather, and there is also a centuries-old service industry, namely the Church. Vic is a bishopric whose diocese extends from the Pyrenees down to the Conca de Barberà, south-west of Barcelona, and is populated with numerous churches, seminaries and convents, all lying within the limits of the old city.

El centre històric will provide you with another of those pleasurable experiences of immersion in history as you wander round the narrow litter-free streets and let your senses feast on the ambiance. It is contained within a clearly defined perimeter, the variously named Ramblas, and you can walk from one end to the other of this pear-shaped old city in twenty minutes although you will need closer to two hours to do it justice. A good starting point is the *Ajuntament*, the town hall, which corners on to the *Plaça Mayor* with its convenient underground car park. Just inside the entrance to the *Ajuntament* is the tourist desk where you can pick up a map of the town and leaflets on buildings of particular interest including one on the Touristic Route of the Historic Centre of Vic, a route which has been signposted for visitors to follow. Before leaving you should ask to visit the rest of this fine building, whose origins date back to 1388. Two of the public rooms are impressive, the *Sala de las Columnas* and the *Sala del Consistori* (the Council Room), with its high-backed crimson leather seats and fine domed roof. Back in the spacious *Plaça Mayor* you can admire the splendid hotchpotch of styles in the façades of the buildings surrounding it, and Josep Pla suggests you stroll under the arches, have a coffee, buy some *pa pessic* (a sort of sweet, cakey bread) and admire the exterior of the *Ajuntament*, 'one of the handsomest buildings in the land'. If an aperitivo appeals more than a coffee and cake you can drop into the 'Bar Montserrat', tucked under the arches, which has an excellent selection of tapas and bocadillos.

Vic is a town famed for its street markets: on Saturdays in the *Plaça Mayor* clothes and items for the home; on the first Saturday in each month a second-hand goods market in the *Plaça dels Martirs*; and, once a year on Palm Sunday, *El Mercat del Ram*, 'The Market of the (olive) Branch', is held in the *Plaça Mayor*, as it has been ever since the Middle Ages. It's massively attended and so perhaps wiser to miss.

However, to see the true dimensions of the *Plaça Mayor* you need to be in Vic on a day when there is no market in the square so that its proportions and the variety of architecture in the surrounding buildings, which include Gothic, Baroque, Renaissance and Moderniste styles, can be appreciated unhindered, and from here you can start your walk round the *Casc antic*, the old city centre.

Starting from the *Plaça Mayor* and following the signposted Tourist Route, leave the square down the *carrer de la Ciutat* which starts just behind the Town Hall. From here on just follow the signs and the route will take you past twenty nine buildings of historical interest. Unless you have the stamina of a marathon runner you probably will not want to stop and see everything on the route so some selection is advisable.

The church of *San Justo* is a good example of sixteenth-century Gothic architecture with a fine Baroque reredos, and through the centuries it has always been the church to one seminary or another. A short distance further on the Tourist route, on the *carrer de la Riera*, you pass the *Casa Galadies*, originally built in 1588 but substantially rebuilt in 1858, which today houses the Municipal Cultural Centre.

Once you reach the *carrer Sant Antoni María Claret* look for the *Convento de la Mercè*, the first example of the Noucentist (literally, 'nineteen hundreds', meaning twentieth century) style in architecture you will see on your tour of Vic. The architect who built the convent in 1929 was Josep María Pericas, and inside is the museum of the order of the Claretian Missionaries containing memorabilia of the founder of the order, Padre Claret.

The cathedral of *St Pere* in the *Plaça de la Catedral* is something of a disappointment. Although it has a striking Romanesque eight-storey bell tower and a crypt dating from the eleventh century the rest was rebuilt at the end of the eighteenth century in Neo-Classical style with jumbo-sized capitals on the columns in the nave. The walls inside are covered in huge murals painted by Josep Maria Sert, an international muralist who is buried in the cathedral; painted in monochromes except for the occasional purple drape the effect is one of soporific sobriety. Sert decorated Lympne Castle in Folkestone and Sir Philip Sassoon's residence in Park Lane as well as other commissions in Italy, France and America. He has no relationship with the other famous Sert, Josep Lluis, the Catalan architect who succeeded Walter Gropius as head of the Faculty of Architecture at Harvard and who designed several internationally recognized buildings in America and Spain. Pla dismisses the cathedral as second class compared to those of Tarragona, Girona and Barcelona.

The Episcopal Museum, considered by Unesco to be one of the most important in Spain for religious art, is right beside the cathedral. It contains an extraordinary collection of Romanesque and Gothic art with examples of all the artistic techniques used in the Romanesque period including what is probably the most representative examples of this period's paintings on wood anywhere in the world. Other rooms display sculpture, archaeological finds, ecclesiastical vestments, leather, ceramics, numismatics and fine gold and silver work. At present the museum is only open in the mornings.

As you follow the route down the Rambla del Bisbar you approach the eleventh-century bridge over the river Mèder, still in use today as a pedestrian crossing over the river; one end of it was badly damaged in 1939 during the Civil War but has been well repaired. The *carrer dels Dolors* leading you back into the old town from the bridge takes you past the church of *els Dolors* with its tiny Baroque interior – all gold leaf – and domed roof. A congregation of more than about thirty would pack the place out.

A little further along these narrow jinking streets you suddenly come across a beautifully proportioned Roman temple and from its excellent condition it obviously must be a recent reconstruction. Originally built in the second century the temple had been 'lost' over the centuries, its walls forming part of the central patio of the eleventh-century castle of the Montcadas, and the remains of the temple were discovered in 1882 when most of what remained of the castle was demolished. The temple was rebuilt and the result is very effective; parts of the original walls have been reconstructed inside and are worth viewing under the finely-judged lighting. What little remains of the castle is just behind the temple and it was here that the King of Catalonia and Aragon, Jaume I, came after conquering Mallorca from the Saracens in 1229 with a fleet of, reputedly, some five hundred ships, an impressive naval force even in modern times.

At the end of the Rambla dels Montcada lie the church and convent of *Santa Teresa*, originally built in 1646 by the architect Josep Morató and home today of the Carmelite nuns. If you can get into the church, which is not always open to the public, you can see the sumptuous Baroque reredos made by Pau Costa at the turn of the seventeenth century, a highly-rated example of the genre. To gain access to the church you enter through the convent's main doorway and a sign invites you to pull on a rope which jangles a bell within. Built into the wall under the rope is a revolving trap door arrangement which enables you to exchange cash for whatever is offered to you by the friendly voice of a nun who answers your call by the bell but remains discreetly out of sight. She will tell you when you can visit the church – currently Saturdays and Sundays – and perhaps offer you some mementos of the convent.

The convent corners on to the *Plaça de las Teresas* which lies at one end of the Rambla del Passeig where Vic's oldest café' – the 'Café Vic' – is located. It has been in the Cuatrecasas family for 145 years and, frankly, gives the impression that it may have been spruced up a couple of times in the nineteenth century but not since. It does however have an impressive variety of coffee and liqueur combinations on offer should your curiosity take you there.

Working your way back along the Tourist route you pass in front of the *Casa Clariana*, originally built in 1509 and well restored, and just beyond and fronting on to the *Plaça de Don Miguel de Clariana* you reach the palatial *Casa Masferrer*, built at the end of the last century and a good if not outstanding example of Moderniste architecture. Currently housed here are the Vic Astronomical Society, a school and several municipal offices, which gives you some idea of the size of the place. The Catalan poet, priest and champion of Catalan Nationalism, Jaume Colell, lived here for a period and you will come across several references to him as you wander round Vic, including a plaque recording a poetic statement on the right to independence:

No captem el dret de viure
Dret que no es compra ni es ven
Poble que mereix ser lliure
Si no li donen s'ho pren

For the right to live we do not make a plea
A right which is neither bought nor sold
A people who deserve to be among the free
Will take freedom for themselves if it's withheld

As you roam round the pedestrian precinct in the central part of the old town, with the smell of freshly-baked bread drifting round a corner of one of the ever narrower streets lined with cozy little shops, and you mingle among people quietly pursuing their daily affairs the thought of acquiring a little pied-à-terre somewhere here seems very appealing.

While you are in the old town you should buy some of Vic's famed *llonganissa*, a variety of pork sausage known as *salchichon* in the rest of Spain. A good shop for all kinds of local *charcuterie* is the 'Xarcuterie Marti' on the *Plaça del Canonge Colell* (the same canon Colell whose little ditty on Catalan freedom appears above) where you can currently buy it for about Ptas 1,500 per kilo.

If you decide to eat in Vic there are some good restaurants serving a variety of food: 'La Taula' in the *Plaça de Don Miguel de Clariana* and 'Basset' on the *carrer San Sadurni*, both in the old part of town, enjoy solid reputations. If you would prefer to eat in a traditional, family inn then 'Ca L'U' is the place to go at no. 4 *Plaça de Santa Teresa*. 'Ca L'U' means, literally, 'the number one house' but the family who run it are not sure how it got its name. The dining room is large and the decor is unusually light and airy for an old established Fonda. There is as wide a choice of food as you would expect and the cooking is sensible and palatable.

This is the sort of establishment in which to try a couple of traditional Catalan dishes so you could start with *escudella*, a broth. It's similar to the *Cocido Madrileño* but has some additional ingredients: *botifarra* (catalan sausage), *mongetes* (white beans) and *la pilota* (a large meatball made of minced meat, bread crumbs, egg and spices). Other ingredients are vegetables, rice, potatoes and noodles. It is always very tasty but don't let anyone talk you into eating a by-product of the broth, called *Carn d'olla* unless you happen to enjoy meat with all of its flavour boiled away and what remains of some over-boiled vegetables; traditionally you eat the *escudella* first and follow it with the cam d'olla, which was boiled with it to give it flavour. After the *escudella,* you could order a plate of *escalivada,* which consists of peeled and grilled sweet red peppers, egg-plants and onions, served with a liberal dosing of oil, some salt and plenty of chopped garlic sprinkled on top. It can be eaten hot or cold, on its own as a first course or as accompaniment to meat or fish, and it is very flavoursome. The sensation as you munch on the very tender smooth and lubricated vegetables is almost as if they have been partially predigested by some tame thing or other kept out of sight in the kitchen, slithering down your throat like the regurgitated morsels fed to its young by a bird of prey. But don't be put off – it really is a very tangy way to eat these basic products from the Catalan countryside.

A good choice of wine to have with the *escudella* would be a *vi novell* from the D.O. Ampurda – Costa Brava or from any other catalan D.O., these being the local version of vin nouveau. If you prefer a quality red wine you could try a bottle of Raimat Abadia from the Costers de Segre D.O., produced by Bodegas Raimat near Lleida and excellent value for the price.

Before starting your return to Girona you can make a short detour to the *Parador* just outside the town and from where you have a splendid view over the Sau reservoir, which is the upper end of the Sau-Susqueda water complex you passed at the start of your day.

Your trip back to Girona will only take you about thirty minutes on the C-25, a new highway built by the Catalan government as part of its overall infrastructure planning for the region. This road provides a fast link between Girona and Lleida so that through traffic from France does not have to go down to Barcelona to pick up the A-7 and then the A-2 motorways to Lleida and beyond. Driving down it from Vic the sensation you have is one of gliding along at tree-top level, the road sweeping up and down the hills and valleys of this densely-forested countryside, occasionally diving into a tunnel and emerging again to magnificent views away over small peaks and the unbroken carpet of trees below. A few tiny hamlets drift past and at one point you get what must be the best view of Les Agudes, the twin crags forming the southern tip of the Montseny mountain and, at 1,706 metres, just six metres lower than the Turó de l'Home itself. Because this road bisects the rugged terrain lying between Girona and Vic so efficiently you also have the choice of making your visit to Vic a separate sortie from the trip to the Vall d'en Bas; the journey between Vic and Girona only takes around thirty minutes.

Girona

Girona is a town full of historic buildings and old streets that curve and wind their way up to the magnificent Gothic cathedral of *Santa Maria de Girona*, built with a single, aisle-less nave on high ground overlooking the city. It is a place to visit on foot and there is such a large number of old buildings to see that you can spend a whole day wandering round the town, if your feet will stand it, soaking up its history and, at strategically timed rest periods, something a little stronger to refuel for the next session.

It is a relatively small town for a capital of a province but it has always been a strategic centre geographically, controlling the strip of land that forms a transition zone between the Pyrenees and the Mediterranean and thus the vital communications between the Iberian peninsula and France and the rest of Western Europe. It is blessed with an abundance of water, four rivers – the Ter, Oñar, Guell and Galligans – converging here, a godsend which has turned into the curse of disastrous floods on an average of eight times per century since the fourteenth century but nevertheless the abundant availability of water was always a factor in the town's prosperity. It was founded by the Romans on the Via Augusta, their main road from Rome to Iberia, and they occupied it for five centuries but all that can be seen of the Roman city today are parts of the walls and defence towers in the cathedral square, at the Gironella tower and to the east of the Sobreportas gate. In those times Girona was a triangular-shaped fortified city lying between the points where today stand the Gironella tower, the *Plaça San Felíu* and the *Placeta del Correu Vell*. The Visigoths, Germanic tribes who invaded Spain in the fifth century after the fall of the Roman Empire, succeeded the Romans and held sway over the area without contributing much to the development of the town or the welfare and progress of its citizens until Charlemagne's army threw them out in 785 and incorporated Girona into the Carolingian empire.

In the eighth century the town expanded outside the walls built by the Romans but the original high part of the city, the area which today lies around the cathedral, was where the clergy and the nobility lived as they would continue to do for centuries to come.

Because of its strategic importance the city has always been the centre of armed conflict between competing armies fighting to control it. It was laid siege to no less than thirty four times between the seventh and nineteenth centuries! In one short period between the end of the eighth century and the beginning of the ninth it changed hands eight times. The last major siege was in 1809 when Napoleon's army laid siege to the town from May to December before occupying it for the next four years and destroying its best defences.

Such is the historical background against which the rich assemblage of old buildings you can visit was compiled over the centuries, and the old part of the city still retains much of its mediaeval character. But before starting your round of visits to some of the more interesting corners it is a good idea to start your tour with a stroll down the Rambla, an attractive, porticoed pedestrian street flanked by burghers' town houses and which runs parallel to the river Ofiar and is a good central point from which to explore the historic quarter. There are frequent street markets on the Rambla so you may be fortunate and coincide with one, which adds to the enjoyment of moving among the townsfolk doing their shopping and chatting to acquaintancies. While on the Rambla buy a street map of the town which labels the historic buildings so that you can plan a route through the maze of old streets.

Although the Romanesque style of architecture had its origins in the eleventh century in Catalonia almost all of the Romanesque buildings in Girona date from the twelfth century, and they are all well preserved. The church of *Sant Pere de Galligans* has an unusual bell tower which is square at first floor level and then rises up another three storeys as an octagon.

Within, the cloister with arches supported on twin columns with elaborately carved capitals is a triumph of good proportions. Close by, at another chapel, the petite *San Nicolás* with its semi-circular apses sitting snugly around its octagonal dome, is another beautiful example of the Romanesque style. The *Banys Àrabs*, the Arab baths, considered a jewel among Girona's historic buildings, also dates from the twelfth century although it was rebuilt in the thirteenth and this is one you certainly should not miss. It is an excellent example of all that makes Moorish architecture in Spain so handsome, exquisite design in the details and mathematically pure proportions in the structural elements in the building, especially as viewed from the inside.

The cathedral is the outstanding example among the Gothic buildings in the town. The original Romanesque cathedral was consecrated in 1038 by Bishop Pedro Roger, brother of the Countess of Barcelona, Ermessinda, but all that remains of this building is the splendid crypt and part of the six-storey bell tower which is known as Charlemagne's Tower and forms a sort of buttress to the Gothic cathedral. Built during the fourteenth and early fifteenth centuries, a long list of famous artisans worked on the fine details inside the building among which is the extraordinary altar-piece of superb repoussé silverwork which took three craftsmen thirty eight years to complete and which is claimed to be the best of its kind in Spain; then there are the glorious stained-glass windows and the finely carved statues and tombs. But it is the sheer size and height of the single nave that most impress the visitor; sixty metres long, thirty four metres high and with a width of twenty three metres, it make it the widest Gothic construction in Europe, according to Josep Pla. The architect responsible for its design was Guillem (William) Bofill. In contrast to the aesthetically severe lines inside, the eighteenth-century Baroque façade at the west end of the nave that looks out over the formal grand stairway, whose ninety six steps you climb up to enter the cathedral, is an unusual addendum to such a monumental Gothic building. It was built by Pedro Costa and one wonders which bishop came up with the idea of plastering a Baroque front on to the end of the nave.

Before leaving, a visit to the cathedral museum, accessed through the cloister, will reward you with a fine display of almost 150 choice pieces of ecclesiastical and other historical objects dating from 975 to the nineteenth century, the most famous of which is the tapestry of the Creation made in the eleventh century.

Other buildings to see are the Episcopal palace, which houses an art museum with Roman sculptures, mediaeval silverwork and Renaissance and Baroque art, and is adjacent to the cathedral on the *Plaça dels Apòstols*; *Sant Pere de Galligans*, formerly a Benedictine monastery with a Romanesque church and cloister which today houses the Archaeological museum; the church of *Sant Feliú*, which combines

Romanesque, Gothic, Ecclesiastical and Military architecture, the latter because it was situated outside the town walls and therefore had to incorporate defences, and, finally, the Dominican monastery on the Rambla de Sant Domènec.

All of this is in the old town, to which the writer, Josep Maria Gironella, awards the perhaps extravagant distinction of being the most authentically preserved mediaeval collection of buildings in Europe. But with its steep narrow streets, tiny squares, and the cathedral bell clock booming out and audible at every corner, and with all the stone-built convents and monasteries and houses of the nobility, the carved doorways and stone-framed windows, and the coats-of-arms and inscriptions engraved on the walls, all relieved sporadically by greenery sprouting from hidden town gardens, this is an especially rewarding experience for the visitor. And it is authentic, with no modern sprucing up of stonework nor revamping of windows and doorways, leaving you to see the place very much as it has always been.

The Jewish quarter (*el Call*) is another component of the charm of Girona. Today, the area around the *carrer de la Força* and adjoining streets is a good example of what the Jewish community enjoyed as their habitat until the decree from the Catholic Monarchs, Ferdinand and Isabel, expelled them from Spain. The quarter was a city within a city, with its own walls, and although the Jews ventured out and traded in the Christian part of town few Christians were allowed into the *Call*. But there was always an undercurrent of resentment and hostility towards the Jews, not unusual when a minority group is seen to be culturally, scientifically and economically superior, quite apart from any religious prejudice and intolerance. All this led to violent attacks on the Jews and attempts to oblige them to convert to Christianity so that from the thirteenth century, when the community enjoyed its greatest brilliance, to the fatal year of 1492 the community was on the decline. The infamous decree arrived in Girona at the end of April and by 31 July, when they had to have left Spanish territory, they had to sell up, inevitably at disastrously low prices. Most of them moved into the neighbouring region of the Rousillon in France.

By now you will be wondering what to eat, your appetite sharpened by the splendours of this town. The province has established a comprehensive programme to control the production of and promote an exceptionally high quality of veal which has its own registered brand, known as *Vedella* (veal) *de Girona.* Eight districts and three municipal authorities award the brand to producers who comply with the procedures laid down for the nurturing and feeding of the livestock to be sold under this quality guarantee. All foodstuffs fed to the cattle must be natural and based on cereals and leguminous beans and peas, apart from milk in the early weeks of the animal's life, and the breeder must keep detailed records of the feeding of his herd. Each animal must have at least two and a half square metres of space to develop in, which doesn't sound much and makes you wonder what a run-of-the-mill calf has to develop in, and they cannot be slaughtered before they reach a specific weight, which they would normally attain at around ten months. Given this quality assurance a veal-based dish might well attract you, and if you like wild mushrooms you could order *Filet de Vedella amb bolets*, fillet of veal with wild mushrooms.

An excellent first course, if you like spinach, is *Espinacas a la Catalana* where the spinach has been lightly fried after boiling, as pine nuts, raisins and tender garlic are added. It is eaten on its own and is as savoury a way of enjoying spinach as you'll find. As an alternative first course a dish of snails, *cargols*, prepared in a sauce with sweet and hot peppers, tender onions and tomatoes makes a flavoursome start to the meal and is popular all over Catalonia. Snails are also one of the ingredients in rabbit cooked with *cigalas* (*escamarlans* in Catalan), the Mediterranean equivalent of a crayfish – *conill amb escamarlans i cargols.*

As you are bordering on the Empordà district you could try a red wine, a Castillo de Perelada Reserva, which is another good wine from the D.O. Empordà – Costa Brava, a touch lighter on the palate at 11.5% than the 12.5% Riojas and a special pleasure if it happens to be the 1978 vintage. Rosé wines are really the forte of this area, though, so any such wine sold under the D.O. seal will be very drinkable.

That standard item for dessert all over Spain, *flan*, a sort of baked custard or cream caramel with a light caramel coating, may appeal to crown whatever went before and if the *flan* is homemade you can be sure you will enjoy it.

So, suitably wined and dined you should be feeling benign and receptive when you have to listen, later in the day, to the golfer's exploits out on the course.

VI

The Pyrenees and the District of La Cerdanya

Real Club de Golf de Cerdaña

In terms of the consummate pleasure to be had playing golf in beautiful surroundings this course is the jewel in the crown of Catalan golf and one of the gems of European golf.

The broad valley of La Cerdanya, one of Europe's most extensive mountain plateaus, lies between the Pyrenees to the north and the imposing Sierra del Cadí on its southern side, the Sierra being the more impressive of the two mountain ranges as seen from the golf course because it rears upwards quite vertically from this vantage point, and although the major peaks of the Pyrenees are higher they are out of your line of sight behind more gently rising ground.

Presumably the founding members of the club inaugurated in the 1930s by the King himself, Alfonso XIII, and hence the 'Real' in the name, were very aware that Madrid disapproved of the Catalan language in general with its separatist connotations, including the use of Catalan spelling in place names, and so called it 'Cerdaña' in the club's official title as against 'La Cerdanya' in Catalan.

The vistas from every corner of the course are so striking that even a totally besotted golfer should feel that perhaps his game is interfering with the views. If you have the good fortune to arrive in May everything is at its best: the crests of the mountains are still covered in snow, incandescent against the blue sky, the trees are displaying that spanking-fresh greenness of spring, and the rough is alight with wild flowers. A trout stream tumbles through one part of the course and the bells of grazing cattle and horses in the adjacent fields keep you company, never silent for a second. You are at an altitude of eleven hundred metres and the air is as clear as the Creator first made it, sharply defining everything in view, and the sun is already warm on your back at this stage in the Pyrenean spring. It would be the perfect place to come and convalesce – perhaps after playing Masia Bach – or even to bid your final '*adios*' to the world.

The clubhouse, a new annex of double-suite bedrooms and the golf shop and store for members' clubs beside the first tee, each building a fine example of the stonemason's art, blend beautifully into the surroundings. Built in slate stone with tones varying from dark grey to russet, with their black slate roofs and varnished wooden window frames, they seem just another element of the countryside, as natural and harmonious as the trees, the grass and the mountains in the background. Why is it that modern construction techniques and materials seem to be incapable of producing buildings like these which visually just melt into the landscape?

Inside, the clubhouse is as charming and cozy as any mountain chalet should be. It is in fact a hotel, 'El Chalet del Golf', and it has been run by Alberto Lucarini and his wife, Rosa, for the last twenty six years. If you stay here you will find the cuisine well above the norm for hotel food. The bedrooms in the hotel itself are somewhat spartan and rather small but the double suites in the annex are roomy and comfortable. The views from all of the bedrooms match those out on the course.

The bar and lounge are wood-panelled and there is a welcoming fireplace in the sitting room. The restaurant is elegantly decorated and looks out over the first, seventeenth and eighteenth fairways with their mountain backdrop. You also have a privileged view of the putting green where you will quite likely see a local member, cigar jammed between his teeth, practising the ancient art of missing the hole. Even if you do not stay in the hotel it is worth having a meal here to enjoy the panorama – and there must be few to rival it anywhere in golf – from a table beside the window; you can sit down to lunch as late as 3.30 p.m.

Your snake charmer of the little white ball should really enjoy this course with something of an old-fashioned feel about it. It is reasonably flat and at 5,726 metres (6,262 yards), par seventy one, does not require him to have the distance off the tee of a professional. Even if the sky is cloudless advise him to take his rainwear with him because you are in the mountains and the weather can change every quarter of an hour, especially if you coincide with an unsettled weather pattern.

The first fairway is like a welcoming doormat, wide enough to land a jumbo jet on it and trouble-free through to the green, 472 metres (516 yards) distant. As you walk down towards it the peak of Tossa d'Alp soars up to 2,531 metres behind the poplars lining the right side of the fairway, with the ski slopes of Masella just visible and another feature of the course is revealed: the very desirable single-storey chalet homes dotted around, built in the same materials as the clubhouse and so well sited – usually slightly lower than the adjacent fairway and surrounded by bushes and shrubs – that they are hardly noticeable, hugging the ground like mushrooms.

The turf on the fairways has a similar texture to that you would find in northern Europe, firm and springy, similar to a moorland heath, and the greens generally have little fall on them and are consistently paced. The variety of trees add to the beauty of the setting and the course is open all year round except for the periods in winter when snow lies on it. The Cerdanya winter is relatively mild for its altitude due to its east-west orientation unlike most of the Pyrenean valleys which run north to south, and this gives it more sunlight hours per day.

The uphill par three fourth hole plays longer than its 189 metres (207 yards) but poses no other problems and from the tee of the fifth hole there is a dramatic view down La Cerdanya towards Andorra, the peaks of the Sierra del Cadí drifting away into the distance forming the horizon on the left, and at shorter range, villages with their stone-built houses clustered round the spires of the churches stand out from the pastures covering the valley.

The seventh hole is the one everyone remembers, its tee located right on the bank of a fast flowing trout river, one of the many in the valley which eventually pour into the river Segre. The hole has a ninety degree dog-leg to the left with the green hidden behind the trees lining the left side of the fairway so it requires playing a mid-iron off the tee, while making a silent plea to the Supreme Golfer to be spared even a suggestion of a slice, which would cast the ball straight at the trout, and if you hit it far enough, about 155 metres (170 yards), the green opens up for a short iron to the flag. The eighth is a picture book par three cut out of the trees with water bordering the green down its left hand side and behind it. The ninth and tenth holes are two of the longer par fours on the course, the tenth green protected by water some thirty metres in front and invisible from the area on the fairway from where you hit your second.

The twelfth is rated the stroke index 1 hole and the long uphill second shot to a well protected green makes it a demanding par four. The fifteenth is a very good par five, requiring a well placed second shot to the right of the fairway to open up the green. The tee-shot on the seventeenth, a 176 metre (192 yard) par three, is played to a green surrounded by trees that would do justice to a botanical garden, a beautiful design by the architect of this layout. The eighteenth is long but wide, the green tucked under the side of the clubhouse where the chairs on the terrace beckon the returning hero to relax and drink in the scenery and, of course, a beer.

X X X

Llivia

La Cerdanya extends into France, the border at Bourg Madame only a couple of kilometres from Puigcerdà, and even though the administration of the valley has alternated historically between France and Spain depending on the outcome of a given scrap between the two it has always been viewed by those living there as a composite whole and there is nothing of note to distinguish either side of the border from the other, except that the French speak Catalan with a hint of a French accent. Llivia is a small Spanish enclave just a few kilometres inside France with no frontier controls when you cross into France and then back into Spain four kilometres further on; if it wasn't for the road signs you would never know that you had momentarily changed countries.

The enclave of Llivia includes two hamlets apart from Llivia itself, Gorguja and Estavar, but it is Llivia which is worth visiting and has a history dating back to the Romans, who made it their centre for controlling La Cerdanya. The Moors were also here in the eighth century before it became the object of various tussles between France and Spain. Carlos V of Spain conceded it the title of *Vila* in 1528 which seems to have favoured it when it was excluded from the list of thirty three villages ceded to the French at the Treaty of the Pyrenees, signed in 1659 to end the war between Felipe IV of Castilla and Catalunya-Aragon and Louis XIV.

The 'Hotel Llivia' makes a good base for a stay in La Cerdanya and if you choose to do so ask for a room on the third floor facing west, which will give you a cinemascope view out through your large window right down La Cerdanya towards Andorra just by sitting up in bed.

In the village itself – you can hardly describe it as a town even if it was given the title of *Vila* – there are several buildings which deserve a visit. The fourteenth-century *Casa de la Vila*, the Town Hall, and the sixteenth-century church of *Santa Maria* are prime buildings, and within the scope of the municipal museum is the eighteenth-century Llivia Pharmacy, reputedly the oldest in Europe, with an important collection of ceramic pots for keeping drugs, herbs and other potions, as well as books and pharmaceutical instruments and a Baroque-style cupboard made by Josep Sunyer and which was also a safe-box for dangerous substances. The museum also has a good collection of ceramics from the period between the tenth and eighteenth centuries.

Can Ventura

It would be a mistake not to eat once at this restaurant located in the centre of the village and housed in an ancient building with a curiously asymmetric shape when viewed from across the street. The restaurant and the little bar beside the entrance share a convincingly rustic-chic ambience, the result of leaving the walls and ceiling in their original condition and of adding furnishings that contrive to add some tone to the place. The cuisine does not pretend to be anything other than Catalan food cooked well, and if you enjoy meat you should try the *carn a la pedra*, (on some menus it is sometimes called *carn a la llosa*), a fillet steak cooked and served on a very hot thick piece of slate which gives the meat a texture all of its own. Trout (*Truita de riu* in Catalan and *trucha* in Spanish) cooked the same way is also good. You could try a Gran Coronas red wine from Bodegas Torres in the Penedès to have with your meat or Blanc de Blancs white wine from Marques de Monistrol, also in the Penedès, with the trout.

Puigcerdà

The main town today in the Spanish part of La Cerdanya is Puigcerdà, close to the border with France. As seen from a distance and indeed as you approach it, you get the impression that there can be little to lure the visitor in to make a closer acquaintance, looking no more than an untidy collection of drab buildings perched on a hill. Once inside, and on foot, some of the character of the place begins to emerge.

Most of what is worth visiting is, as you will have guessed, in the old town, the *vila vella*. You could start at the *Plaça Mayor*; the old, central square, with its burghers' houses and the *Ayuntament*, the Town Hall. You can also have a grand panoramic view down the valley from a viewing point in the square. The bell tower of the church of *Santa Maria* should also impress you as you squint up its forty two metres, and the old hospital still contains part of a previous building in a transitionary style between Romanesque and Gothic.

Walking round the central shopping streets you soon feel the sense of homeliness of a small town community living remote from any big city even if you also instinctively know that it could, depending on the individual, soon induce intense claustrophobia if you were obliged to stay here for a long period.

Pla found the lake within the confines of the town quite romantic but today, apart from some fine houses bordering it and gone to seed, it is no better than similar ones in many medium-sized European cities, a definite asset for the citizens to stroll round on a summer's evening but not worth the purchase of a postcard for the family.

From Puigcerdà you can head off westwards down La Cerdanya and visit some of the unspoilt villages sited randomly along the length and breadth of the valley. The geological origin of the area was a lake formed in the Miocene some ten million years ago and it has been inhabited ever since the Bronze Age. One prehistoric find, the bones of humans found at the Dolmen d'Oren near the village of Prullans, has a feature which still puzzles anthropologists: these were people who were two metres tall!

Bolvir

When you leave Puigcerdà, take the N-260 road in the direction of Andorra and some five kilometres on you arrive at the village of Bolvir, documented more than a thousand years ago as belonging to the monastery of *Sant Miquel de Cuixà* and with traces of a settlement by an Iberian tribe close by, dating from the second/first centuries BC, and one of the few found in the Pyrenees.

The village is a mixture of a bit of everything. It has a mediaeval centre surrounded by stone-built farmers' houses and spreading outwards modern apartments and holiday homes cater to skiers and summer holidaymakers. As in all of La Cerdanya the economy today revolves mainly around farming, mostly dairy farming, and tourism which in turn fuels construction. Tourism in La Cerdanya has developed strongly since the 1960s when improved communications opened the valley up as a recreational area to the the densely-populated province of Barcelona and to France and the rest of Europe to the north. The Cadí tunnel, inaugurated in 1984, made it readily accessible by car from the south and the recently completed Puigmorens (Puymorens to the French) tunnel has done the same from France.

The twelfth-century church of *Santa Cecilia* with its slate roof dominates the old centre and has a striking south-facing doorway of recessing arches on slim columns, each with a finely chiselled capital; the spire of the church is a later addition. The street leading up to the church entrance is still paved with rough hewn stones making it look much as it must have done in mediaeval times. A curious detail from the past is the meadow called *Pla de la mala mort* where traditionally cattle are forbidden to graze because the Viscount of Cerdanya is said to have killed one of his enemies there, hence the name – The meadow of the bad death.

Torre del Remei

On the outskirts of Bolvir and standing in two hectares of garden lies the 'Torre del Remei', an elegant mansion built in Moderniste style which today is a luxury hotel with an excellent restaurant and a member of the Relais & Chateaux organization. This striking building dates from 1910 when a Barcelona banker, Agustí Manaut i Taberner, commissioned a well regarded local architect from Llivia, Sr Freixa, to build a country retreat for his daughter, Blanca, to assuage a bad conscience after dipping in to her private funds to stave off a financial crisis at the bank. The result, at least as seen today after modernization of the facilities inside the building, is an impeccable example of Moderniste architecture.

When Josep-Maria Boix and his wife Loles purchased the by then empty building in 1988 they placed the responsibility for modernizing and enlarging the original building in the hands of an architectural design office in Barcelona who were instructed to ensure that the Moderniste style, which, naturally, encompassed all the interior details, was scrupulously maintained. The result is a visual feast for the dilettante guest in the opulent surroundings of a luxury hotel of singular character where style, good taste and fine cuisine are the signature of a remarkable establishment.

The guest accommodation is limited to eleven suites, each quite different from the others in size, shape, furnishings and decor but all sharing ravishing views of the mountains, whirlpool baths, thermostatically controlled under-floor heating in the marble-floored bathrooms as well as all the modern electronic trappings you would expect in an establishment of this category. Each room is named after the dominant feature visible from the bedroom window – *Tossa d'Alp, Pla de la Boira, Puig de Coma Dolça, Riu dels Estanys* and so on. Prices per room and per day currently range from Ptas 60,000 for the Suite Principal, which has a bathroom that could accommodate a rugby team, down to Ptas 25,000 for the smaller rooms. The hotel is always full at the weekends so you need to book at least a week or two ahead for a weekend stay and several months in advance if you wish to book for any days in August.

The hotel's extensive garden is an invitation to an early morning or a late evening saunter under centenarian trees with glimpses of the Sierra del Cadí through the leaves, and to enjoy an inspection of the vegetables, herbs and fruit trees in the kitchen garden which provides many of the raw materials used by the chefs.

Even if you do not make the hotel the base for your stay the restaurant, of a calibre of its own in La Cerdanya, deserves a visit. The cuisine reflects the skills of Josep-Maria Boix who has cooked for several members of European royalty on their official visits to Spain and who won the National Gastronomy prize in 1987 for the best individual chef. The elegant dining room complements the cuisine so somehow, whatever his fortune out on the course, you must make it plain to the golfer that a meal here is a condition of allowing him to continue to indulge his golf – or better, if you start manoeuvring with this strategy back home when still in the planning stage of the trip you could make a two-night stay at the 'Torre del Remei' your condition for agreeing to the golfing holiday.

If you do eat there you would have an opportunity to try one of Josep Maria Boix's versions of some local dishes, such as hare prepared with beans and garnished with asparagus tips and a type of wild mushroom – *rossinyols*. A Sangre de Toro from Bodegas Torres or a Perelada Reserva would be suitable company for the hare.

Golf Fontanals de Cerdanya

What makes a trip to La Cerdanya so rewarding from the golfer's point of view is that there are two excellent courses only fifteen minutes or so apart with the Fontanals course complementing the one at the Real

Club de la Cerdaña. Fontanals was opened in 1994 and today is unquestionably one of the quality courses in Catalonia. Designed on what was previously flat pasture land, the course has few natural features to distinguish one hole from another so the designer has created several lakes to add visual interest as well as challenges in shot execution.

The overall character of the course is decidedly American with fine white sanded bunkers everywhere, a hundred in total, making it by far the most bunkered course in the region. It is also the longest at 6,159 metres (6,735 yards) and par seventy two from the yellow tees. From the white tees it runs 6,454 metres (7,058 yards) and has an SSS of seventy four! One hole, the par four fifteenth, has no less than nine bunkers on it. Still, the sand is fine, soft and deep so green-side bunker shots are controllable. A bird's-eye view from above would look as though someone had scattered large white clover leafs all over the place because the designer seems to have been of a mind that that's the only shape for any bunker worthy of the name.

Two things are immediately evident when you first make acquaintance with Fontanals: the high standard of quality in every detail out on the course and the excellent level of maintenance. Another feature is found in the little streams, beautifully channelled in natural stone, running through many of the holes and which are there to drain off the water coming into the valley from the surrounding mountains and run it eventually into the Segre. On some holes they pass under the fairways and on others they are exposed, ready to catch your ball which, if you're not sharp enough off the mark in pursuit, will be washed away by the fast flowing water, and in the rough they are always open to the skies and wayward golf balls. Unless the golfer plays with a local member he is going to lose one or more balls until he gets to know the course of these little rivulets.

Scenically Fontanals has the same sublime setting as the Real Club de Golf de la Cerdaña and in ten to fifteen years' time, when the newly planted trees have started to mature, it will be as visually satisfying as the older club and, as it is today, a more severe test of golf.

The practice range is, simply, the best this golfer have seen anywhere, a vast tract of quality turf where probably a quarter of the club's members could fire off balls comfortably at the same time.

Your Lord of the Sward will soon become the Seigneur of the Sand if he doesn't have his driving blinkers on as he takes on Fontanals' rather narrow fairways, tightly bunkered to catch different length drives, and he will need to put these on the fairways to have a chance of getting home in regulation on some of the par fours which average 344 metres (376 yards), as well as the par fives, two of which are close to 550 metres (601 yards). The first hole, a par four of 362 metres (396 yards), sets the regime for the day: he will need a very straight tee-shot to avoid the bunkers, with anything wild to the right finishing out-of-bounds, and then the shot to the green, which like all of them on this course is on the small side, must clear the front bunkers. The quality of grass on the fairways gives consistently good lies and the rough is not over-punishing.

The third hole, 384 metres (420 yards), is the first on which a lake intervenes and it is not visible from the fall of the drive; it pays to walk up and take one's bearings before playing the second shot. The 184 metres (201 yards) par three eighth, with a tightly bunkered green, is a serious challenge when the wind is against you. The sixteenth, 363 metres (397 yards), rated the handicap-three hole, will tax anyone's skills when they play their second shot at a green with layers of bunkers in front and a lake running up its right side and then curling round behind it; the conservative tactic is to aim the second shot at the two bunkers which edge up to the left of the green. The final hole, a par four of 378 metres (413 yards) running uphill to the green is the one-handicap hole and once again requires an accurately placed drive to avoid the rivulet on the right and the lake on the left.

Regardless of how he has played your golfer will have enjoyed his day on this beautifully constructed layout in outstanding surroundings, and so, whatever his score, he will be at the very least amiable company for you if you choose to share with him the pleasure of a post-round soother.

X X X

Bellver de Cerdanya
Some fifteen kilometres further down the N-260 from Bolvir you arrive at Bellver de Cerdanya, the largest village in the district and located right on the banks of the Segre. The old centre perched on a hill above the river is visible from all sides as you approach the village and is

where you should head for when you arrive. Unless it is high summer you can usually park in the heart of the old part of the town which saves you quite a slog up the hill.

Beliver was founded in 1225 and its mediaeval centre as seen today must be very much as it was in those times, narrow stone-paved streets surrounded by stone-built houses, with the streets slaloming down the sharply sloping ground. As you wander round, the villagers inhabiting these ancient buildings, which nowadays have all the modern amenities, go about their day's business seemingly oblivious to the presence of strangers. Make sure you do not miss the *Plaça Mayor* and the church of *Santa María i Sant Pere* which towers over the rest of the village.

Hotel Boix, Martinet de Cerdanya

Josep Maria Boix, the owner and inspiration behind the 'Torre del Remei', was born in Martinet and started his career in the catering business in Barcelona where he worked in the kitchens of various hotels before being apprenticed to a celebrated chef at the 'Hotel Colón', Ignasi Domenèch. Later, he and his wife, Loles, opened their own establishment in Martinet, the forerunner of their present hotel, the 'Hotel Boix', just outside the village.

The restaurant of the 'Hotel Boix' deserves a special mention. Before the 'Torre del Remei' opened for business gourmets from Andorra to Barcelona anticipated their next meal here with as much anticipation and desire as a tired camel-train making for an oasis. The comfortable dining room has that unmistakable look of the professional approach to fine eating, everything *'comme il faut'* but no extravagant distractions to detract from the food so that as you sit down and eye the scene you sense immediately that you are in for a serious culinary experience. Loles is there to welcome you and explain some of the mysterious descriptions on the menu, and there could be no better adviser of what to try if you are in doubt about the local specialities.

If you decide to eat à la carte there is a whole page of appetizers including a salad of *Xicoies* when in season (mid-April to the end of May). *Xicoies* are a small crab-like green plant which grows wild in the area and looks like something between a fern and a crinkly lettuce, and has a stimulatingly bitter tang. It is served with a vinaigrette sauce, nuts, cured duck's-meat and black olives. In the fish section are river trout, hake, grilled salt cod served with *all-i-oli*, squid and fresh tuna fish, and among the meats breast of duck with honey, roast lamb seasoned with mountain herbs, chicken in different styles, ox-tail, rabbit, pig's trotters and pigeon.

Alternatively you can choose between the *Menú clàssic* and the *Menú degustació*. On a recent visit the *Menú clàssic* consisted of an appetizer, a salad of lettuce, sardines and tender onions in a garlic vinaigrette sauce, an entrée of ox-tail cooked with olives, a glass of red wine, homemade ice cream, Catalan almond wafers and, finally, chocolate bonbons, all for Ptas 3,745. The *Menú degustació* listed a 'Boix' hot appetizer, a cold cream of courgette soup with a cheese dressing, tender broad beans cooked Catalan-style, roast fillets of leg of lamb with potatoes peasant-style, a bottle of red wine, bisquit glacée with a chocolate sauce, a hot apple tart with a pear sauce, almond wafers, and chocolate bonbons, at a price of Ptas 5,200.

The hotel as such has a three-star rating and is priced, perhaps, a touch on the high side, and it does not have the broad vistas that are so much a part of La Cerdanya nearer to Puigcerdà but it is a very comfortable establishment and the food will erase the price of the room from your memory.

Trout fishing on the Segre

The Segre above and below Martinet is a favourite stretch of river for trout fishermen so if the scourge of the hard, dimpled ball also fancies himself as a fly fisher or if you count this among your numerous skills, then this is a good opportunity to enjoy this sport provided you coincide with the season which lasts from early May to the end of August. The business of acquiring all the necessary permits could, I suspect, take most of a morning and will, incidentally, get you acquainted with a significant section of the local business community. You need a fishing licence, obtainable in the Bazar Vigo, and you also need a daily permit, which you negotiate for in the Bar Rosaleda. Armed with these you then make your way to Casa Punti in Bellver de Cerdanya where you acquire your special permit to fish this stretch of the river. And some people complain about the Brussels bureaucracy!

The villages of Talló, Oloptc and All

Each of these little villages, all within a short drive from Bellver de Cerdanya, has a Romanesque church that merits a visit. *Santa Maria de*

Talló dates from the twelfth century and has a porch-like entrance made up of three arches. In Olopte the church of *Sant Pere* has an entrance of archivolts supported by columns with capitals decorated with carvings of foliage, and at All, the church of *Santa Maria*, built in the first half of the twelfth century, still displays part of the ironwork used in the original doors and you can admire the Romanesque carvings in the stone surrounds to the entrance done in the typical bas-relief and unadorned simplicity that makes them so similar to figures in modern naif art.

As you walk round these villages the predominant smells are of hay and cows and most of the streets bear traces of cow dung from cattle returning in the late afternoons to be milked in the cow sheds. For urbanites and suburbanites it's all pungently rural.

Can Borrell in Les Meranges

Les Meranges is a small village lying at the 1,540-metre level which makes it the highest in La Cerdanya, some ten kilometres above Ger on the N-260, which would be your starting point to get there. This is a quite unspoilt Pyrenean village where you will quickly forget the bustle of the modern world as the hours pass by at about half the rate they do anywhere else. It is an ideal centre for walking, cross-country skiing, fishing and horse riding, and there are some interesting flora and fauna to be seen. Among the galaxy of wild flowers that grow profusely in the Toba valley, which lies just below Les Meranges and the neighbouring hamlet of Girul, is the Edelweiss, and herbs, wild strawberries and several different varieties of wild mushroom including the *rovelló, cep* and *fredolic*, all grow in the area. The upper end of the Toba valley down which the Duran river runs, although at this altitude it is no more than a stream, is as idyllic as you will find, with the 2,482-metre *Coll de les Mulleres* closing it out to the north. In the woods and on the peaks antelopes (*rebecos*), deer, a species of woodcock called a capercaillie in English, and the white partridge, which changes colour from grey to white when snow lies on the ground, are among the animal life.

Almost seven hundred metres above Les Meranges there is a lake, *l'Estany de Malniu*, which can be approached by car over a rough track leaving about half an hour's walk to the lake itself, and from there you get a good view of he 2,911-metre peak of Puigpedrós. If you prefer to walk all the way it is about ten kilometres but it is a steep climb.

In Les Meranges itself water, coursing down in rivulets from the mountains behind, runs everywhere so that at night you sleep to a steady tinkling as it falls away to the valley below. Most of the streets are just wide enough for a tractor to pass through and you can walk round the stone-built houses in less than fifteen minutes. The church dedicated to *Sant Sadurní* and *la Mare de Déu de l'Ajuda* dominates the village and you can arrange to visit it by calling at Cal Gispert. Inside, stark simplicity prevails apart from some traces of Romanesque paintings recently discovered on one of the walls.

'Can Borrell' is a small hotel and restaurant founded twenty five years ago by Jaume Guillen, who cleverly converted four village houses into a hotel and restaurant. The present owner, Antonio Forn, added some improvements so that today 'Can Borrell' is a small and cozy country inn of considerable charm and is a member of the French 'Relais du Silence' organization, one of only six listed for Spain and Andorra in their guide. To qualify as a member a hotel has to include these attributes: 'A natural and peaceful environment... comfortable buildings of character... a warm welcome, stressing the quality of life and gastronomy, assured by the personal attention of the owners themselves who know how to make guests feel at home while still being entirely professional'.

At 'Can Borrell' Sr Forn's daughter, Laura, who on first acquaintance seems altogether too young and wispy to fill the shoes of manager but who turns out to be prodigiously competent, is the heart and soul of the place aided by her sister, Alicia, and the rest of the staff, none of whom appear any older than the sisters. Apart from dealing with guests in any one of four languages Laura supervises reservations and the accounts, and is also the Head Chef, and this in a restaurant which enjoys an enviable reputation throughout La Cerdanya. The food justifies the trip up to the village for a meal even if you do not stay the night. If you do decide to stay here the rooms are simple but adequate and the general ambience is one of rustic comfort, with the original stone walls still exposed on the inside of the building. Remember not to leave your bedroom window open for long if you want to avoid the farmyard smells encamping for the night. The large restaurant has a lot of character and an unbeatable view straight down the valley across to the Sierra del Cadí.

The hotel only has eight bedrooms so you should book well in advance on 972-880033. The cost of a double room is currently Ptas 7,490 per night, including tax but excluding breakfast. The hotel and restaurant are only open on Fridays, Saturdays and Sunday lunchtime from 6 January to 30 April. The rest of the year the establishment is closed from Monday night to Wednesday morning.

La Seu d'Urgell and Andorra

As you head westwards La Cerdanya ends just beyond Martinet but you are within twenty five kilometres of the town of La Seu d'Urgell, where one of the largest and most imposing of Romanesque churches in Catalonia is an architectural experience you would regret missing. It is in fact a Cathedral, dedicated to *Santa Maria de Urgell*, and is considered one of the best examples of Lombard Romanesque, the term used to define early Romanesque construction. Building was started in 1040 by bishop St Ermengol on the site of a previous Carolingian church but construction did not finish until the twelfth century. As was customary at the time the altar and main entrance faced east to the Holy Land. As seen from the outside, this monumental example of Romanesque architecture includes in one massive building not only the cathedral but also the church of *St Miquel* and the Episcopal Palace and, large though it is, its principal features are the finely balanced proportions and purity of line.

Inside the cathedral you can see several Romanesque carvings including the Virgin of Andorra from the thirteenth century and the fourteenth-century tombs of Pedro II the Great, who lived from 1240 to 1285 and who had secured the throne of Sicily for the Catalo-Aragonese throne by marrying its princess, Constanza; of Jaume II the Just, king of Aragon and one of Jaume I's sons; of Blanca de Navarra, 1385-1441, daughter of Carlos III of Navarra and, after marrying Martin de Aragón, queen of Sicily; and of Admiral Roger de Llúria, 1250-1305, one of the most successful military men in the history of Spain whose naval skills were only surpassed by his ferocious cruelty on his conquered opponents. Also on display are various relics, chalices and two tenth-century codices.

In the town you can enjoy the *casc historic* with its porticoed streets and the fifteenth century *Ajuntament*, built in Civil Gothic style where you can see some fine paintings and visit the town's archives.

There are only three convincing reasons for continuing on to Andorra from La Seu d'Urgell – either to ski, or to indulge in some duty-free and Vat-free shopping, or to continue on into France. Forget any ideas you may have of a romantic enclave high up in the mountains. The main town of Andorra La Vella is the equivalent of one long shopping mall, and while you can admittedly purchase some things at bargain prices you must be prepared to put up with the crowds and commercialism of the place. If you plan to make your visit in the high summer you should arrive at the border before 9 a.m. to avoid the long line of vehicles which first have to queue to pass the customs and frontier controls and then form another slow-moving line which churns its way up to Andorra La Vella. All of this gets worse as the morning progresses. Prior to Andorra obtaining its own constitution and independence in 1993, an event which made Catalan an official language at the United Nations, it was jointly governed by the President of the French Republic and the Bishop of La Seu d'Urgell, and formally they are still the joint Heads of State. The town has an ancient history and even suffered at the hands of the Moors who devastated it in 784 on their retreat after the battle of Poitiers where their drive northwards into Europe was finally halted.

VII

El Penedès, Montserrat and Sitges

Club de Golf Masia Bach

If the golfer thought that Golf Girona was a severe test of his physical endurance you can warn him that it was just a gentle stroll through the woods compared to what awaits him at Masia Bach. It would be interesting to know José María Olazabal's first reaction to the terrain the founders of the club showed him when they commissioned him to design an eighteen-hole course there. Quite probably they would have given him his first view of it by helicopter because one can't imagine there would have been any other means of working one's way round the abrupt ravines, vertical rock faces and arid patches of stony ground, home to the occasional snake and lizards basking in the sun. That anyone could have contrived to lay out eighteen holes in such unpromising topography is surprising in itself but that the result should turn out to be a demanding, varied and very testing golfing challenge reflects on the skills of the designer. Masia Bach is not most people's idea of a fine golf course: it is too difficult and physically tiring for any but the fit young low-handicapper. A golfing friend rates difficult courses on an ascending scale of three: testing, very difficult and Masia Bach. But it is a course to experience at least once, preferably in a golf buggy, and it will remain a benchmark for the rest of one's golfing life against which to measure other monster courses.

It lies some twenty five kilometres west of Barcelona right on the edge of the district of the Alt Penedès, which together with the neighbouring Baix Penedès is the champagne-growing area of Catalonia. After you leave the A-7 motorway heading south out of Barcelona at Martorell take the road signposted to Capellades, and shortly after passing the turn-off for St Esteban de Sesrovires you will see the entrance to the club on your right. As you drive along you are already in vineyards, just a few of those making up the vast wine-growing area of the Penedès, which is one of the three major quality Spanish wine-producing regions, the others being

Jerez and Rioja. As you park your car beside the clubhouse two nearby features stand out: to the north-west the mountain of Montserrat and, to the east, the imposing chateau-like building of the Masia Bach winery.

Depending on your taste in architecture you may consider the large clubhouse a masterpiece or a disaster piece but what few would dispute is that it blends in with the landscape about as well as an oil-tanker would if sited in the same place. At least the restaurant makes the most of the views, and one has to suppose that the architect was a man who believed in spacious passage-ways because about twenty percent of the building seems to consist of them. Marvellous use of space!

You had better be very, very affectionate and sweet as you say goodbye to the master golfer as he heads out for the first tee because this farewell is just as full of impending drama as that of wives seeing off the troops embarking for the front. He may be lucky and return to you later in the day as one of the walking wounded but in any case, by the time you meet up again you are going to find him shell-shocked after his battle with Masia Bach. And who knows? – he may even renounce golf forever, which would be a shame if you haven't yet completed your tour of Catalonia.

The par five first hole is the antithesis of the character of the rest of this 6,039 metre (6,604 yard) course; its broad fairway runs gently downhill, Montserrat looming in the middle distance to the left and the twin spires of the church of *St Esteban de Sosrovires* lining up behind the green, and with only an out-of-bounds vineyard bordering the right-hand side to worry about as the golfer plays the tee-shot. The green, like all the greens on the course, is tightly bunkered but he would be disappointed not to make par.

The second hole, a par three, deserves a special mention because there is no way a beginner could conceivably get to the green without losing at least one ball unless his Guardian Angel hits it for him. As you stand on the tee, possibly feeling the onset of vertigo, a vast deep void separates you from the green 153 metres (167 yards) in front of you. There is nothing in between except for a metre of bunker just in front of the green, carved out of the other side of the chasm. If your ball disappears somewhere into the hole you walk down a path which crosses a dam forming the lake to the left, and is, therefore, well above the ravine, to a dropping zone quite close to the green and play your next shot, just a short pitch. Asked how beginners play the hole a local member replied that some of them walk straight to the dropping zone without playing the tee-shot, taking the penalty stroke but at least avoiding the loss of a ball.

The climb up from the second green to the third tee is a sample of things to come. It is an extremely steep, rather long trek and the golfer will need some time to recover his breath before he can contemplate dispatching his drive up the third fairway which also climbs away in front of the tee. These feats of mountaineering between greens and tees are frequent all over the course, and as the third hole is uphill all the way and the fourth climbs steeply from the fall of the drive, by the time he stands on the fifth tee he will be feeling about as lively and full of fun as though he had just scaled Everest without oxygen. And he still has thirteen holes to go!

The par four sixth is the stroke index 1 hole and whatever he does, he must avoid hitting his second to the left of the green if he does not want to hole-out in double figures. The seventh is a splendid downhill par five measuring 501 metres (548 yards) which, even if you only half cream your drive, is reachable in two down the steeply sloping fairway.

The eighth is a modest 284 metre (311 yard) par four but it is not ranked the number five handicap hole for nothing. One young professional considers it the hardest par four in Catalonia because although he and other long-hitters are capable of driving the green, the landing area, which is laid almost at right angles to the line of the fairway, is only about four metres deep at the widest point and there is water in front of it and severe trouble behind. For the average handicapper it is advisable to sacrifice length and play an iron off the tee and, hopefully, avoid the lake on the left and the out-of-bounds on the right, both running all the way to the green. The second shot is best played just to the right-hand side of the front of the green from where par can be saved with a chip and a putt.

There is another major mountain climb up to the ninth tee and the same again to the tenth which, if his lungs and legs are still capable of carrying on, is a relatively tame par five. The eleventh plays uphill all the way too but the drive on the twelfth is a case of launching the ball into a valley way below the tee, producing some exciting yardage if the golfer really connects and a chance to get his breathing back to normal as he wanders down to it. He must keep his ball below the flag on his approach otherwise he will three-putt this steeply sloping green.

Unless he is a low handicapper or enjoys playing a golfing version of
Russian roulette he should not attempt to clear the deceptively short-
looking copse that lies between the ball and the stretch of fairway
running to the green after the tee-shot on the thirteenth, a par five.
Everyone plays chicken on their second shot, aiming out to the right of
the tree-filled hazard but still getting within range of the green. There is
still some climbing to be done on the par three fourteenth and the
eighteenth plays uphill all the way but at least the bar is in sight.

X X X

The Cordoníu champagne cellars
Reputedly a monk, Dom Perignon, whose job it was to oversee his
monastery's cellar at Hautvillers in the Champagne district, was the one
to whom succeeding generations owe their gratitude for developing
some three hundred years ago the process which converts white wine
into the delightful drink that universally symbolizes a grand celebration.
Cava is the generic trade name for Spanish champagne, and is in fact the
Catalan word for cellar, where this bubbly wine is matured. The French
were given the exclusive right to use the term 'Champagne' just as the
Spanish were for 'Sherry', or 'Vino de Jerez'. Previously, Spanish
producers labelled their product Champagne but once the international
court's ruling was made they were obliged to come up with a new term
and invest heavily in publicity; even the inclusion of the phrase
'*methode champenoise*', a term which defines the process of producing a
second fermentation in the bottle and which in turn produces the fizz in
the wine, is precluded so some Spanish producers get round this by
using the term '*methode traditionelle*' on their labels. The massive export
figures for *cava* show that the marketing strategy has paid off.

Ninety nine per cent of *cava* is produced in Catalonia and more than
seventy five per cent of the total in the small town of Sant Sadurni
d'Anoia where the Cordoníu cellars are located. Sant Sadurni d'Anoia
lies on l'Anoia, a small river skirting the town, in the heart of the district
of the Alt Penedès and only some twelve kilometres from its capital,
Vilafranca del Penedès. As you approach the town you find yourself
driving through a forest of signs giving the names of all the different
producers of *cava* whose cellars are within the municipal limits. It seems
unreal that such a modest little place should be home to so many firms

dedicated to one of life's luxury drinks but it was here that the Spanish wine industry, at the hands of José Raventós i Fatjó as president and owner of the Cordoníu business, began its adventure in 1872 in the world of this most famous of sparkling wines, and in the business of making fine wines location is, arguably, the most important ingredient of success: if the originator did it here the rest were quick to get the same place name on their labels.

The Cordoníu family's involvement with wine goes back even further than Dom Perignon: in 1551 Jaume Cordoníu founded the family wine business that today, seventeen generations later, is the oldest name in *cava*. The last of the Cordoníu family to bear the name was Ana, who had inherited the business in the seventeenth century and married a Raventós, and the Raventós family still own the company today with several other leading Catalan wineries under their control, including Masia Bach and Raimat as well as the Cordoníu cellars in Nappa valley in California.

The enjoyment of the day starts as soon as you arrive at the Cordoníu premises: Don José Raventós had excellent taste in architecture as well as fine wines and so commissioned Josep Puig i Cadalfalch, the author of the *Casa Amatller* on the 'discordant city block' on *Passeig de Gracia* in Barcelona, to design the buildings for the winery which was to produce *cava*. Of the trio of most famous Moderniste architects Puig i Cadalfalch was the one who most insisted that buildings should reflect their local origins, and there was nothing quite so '*clar i català*' – clear and Catalan – as brick, which was made from the very earth of Catalonia. The Cordoníu buildings are a stunning example of what a gifted designer can do when he applies his talents to what are essentially industrial buildings. Today none of the original buildings performs the functions for which it was designed but they stand there in the spacious and tranquil grounds of the Cordoníu domain, open for the visitor to wander through and admire. The reception building, the first you access, with its hyperbolic arches formed of brick sets the aesthetic standard for all that is to follow. And the Cordoníu organization makes your visit a memorable experience, every detail reflecting devotion to quality and good taste.

If your visit coincides with the grape harvesting season, roughly from the end of August until late October, you will see all the hustle and bustle of the arrival and pressing of the grapes. But outside this season

Cordoníu still make your visit a rich experience: at the hand of an English-, French- or German-speaking guide you will be taken on a tour of the bottling plants prior to what for many is the most memorable part of the tour, a trip through some of the twenty five kilometres – yes! – of cellars, some as much as 25 metres under the ground, in which the gradual process of producing fine *cava* takes place. Quality *cava* is never less than three years in the making and should not exceed five, which requires enormous areas of cellar space – in Cordoníu enough to hold 100 million bottles. *Cava* does not improve with age in the bottle and so should be drunk within a year or so of purchase.

At the end of your visit you will be invited to sample a glass of one of the *cava*s and the guide will explain the different types, all strictly controlled, as are the production methods, by a Regulatory Authority of the industry. The sweetest *cava* is '*semi sec*' (semi dry) and is best enjoyed with a dessert. Then, in ascending order of dryness, you have *sec*, *brut* and *brut natur*. Several types of grapes are used in making *cava* as is the case with French champagne, and it is the art of the oenologist to blend the wines from these varieties of grape to produce just the right flavour for a given brand. *Cava* deserves a place at any meal, either as an aperitif, to drink with light dishes and particularly shellfish, or to finish off the meal. And if your mood is romantic a glass of chilled *cava*, sipped slowly out on a terrace under a summer moon, may even seduce the golfer into taking an interest in something other than his putter.

A morning spent on such hedonic matters clearly requires something special by way of a meal so today you can forget calçots, barbecued onions and perhaps the best known speciality of the Penedès, which are eaten at restaurants equipped with large outdoor grills on which the onions are grilled over a fire of vine cuttings prior to being eaten messily by hand at the grill side, flavoured with a local '*Romescu*' sauce and washed down by liberal quantities of wine drunk straight from the *porrón*. *Calçots* are better enjoyed as a group activity which increases the all-round hilarity as fingers and faces become ever blacker as a result of peeling off the outer singed skin of the *calçot* prior to dipping it in the strong sauce and downing it, head to the sky, by sucking the tender centre of the onion held above your face off its leaves. As an activity, it is a great unwinder of anyone normally on the stiff and reserved side.

Chicken is the staple ingredient for many dishes in the area, usually described as *gall del Penedès* on menus, and either *gall a l'ametlla*, chicken with almonds, or *gall amb champinyons*, chicken with mushrooms, will be representative of what the local cooks can do with a chicken. If you decide to eat in Vilafranca del Penedès you could do so at 'Airolo' on the Rambla de Nuestra Senyora, where a warm salad of diced duck sweetbreads and prawns would set the meal off in style to be followed perhaps by their *suprema de merluza al blanco Penedès*, hake in a Penedès white wine sauce. A bottle of a good Penedès white wine, perhaps a Renè Barbier 'Kraliner' or an Extrisimo Bach sec, would complement the hake.

Els Castellers and the Sardana

If there is one traditional folk activity which characterizes the two districts of El Penedès it is *Els Castellers*, meaning human towers made of layers of people standing on the shoulders of those below them, similar to the stunts of acrobats in a circus who manage to stand one on another up to four persons high. In the case of the *Castellers*, though, towers of nine levels of people are achieved, and this is one of the core attractions in the annual fiesta in every town. The origins of *Els Castellers* goes back to the eighteenth century although the first written reference to them was in 1805 and refers to two teams, called *colles* in Catalan, from the town of Valls, the cradle of the tradition. Today, there are *colles* all over Catalonia, and such is the competitiveness of the activity that teams do regular serious training in halls equipped to allow the members of a *coll* to perfect their techniques. Children are important members of a squad because they make up the top levels of a tower and run the most risk of injury in the event of the tower collapsing, which it frequently does. The fact that serious injury seems to be a rare occurrence must be because those falling are cushioned by the rows of team members forming a human buttress round the base of the tower at ground level. Most towns have their annual fiesta in the summer when the performance of *Castellers* is at its height, and if you are fortunate in coinciding with such an event you will find it full of atmosphere and a very entertaining spectacle with the uncertain outcome of the venture – these towers are even less stable than a house made of cards – adding a touch of drama. The tradition continues to grow in popularity with extensive media coverage of the leading *colles*, some of whom even have web sites on the internet!

You do not have to find a town with its annual fiesta in full swing to see a *Sardana*, the region's folk dance, because this is such a popular phenomenon that the *Sardana* is danced in virtually every village on Sundays and other holidays. Compared to, say, the *Jota* from Aragon or *Sevillanas* from Andalucia, the *Sardana* is rather tame stuff, sedately hopped rather than danced by groups of people in circles holding hands to the accompaniment of somewhat shrill traditional tunes from the local band. To the uninitiated its chief virtue seems to be the spontaneity with which everyone joins in: once the band starts up passers-by dump their bags, coats, jackets and whatever else hinders the dancing in a pile in the middle of the circle they form, and start dancing. Although the overall pace is distinctly unhurried the footwork looks intricate, not that much movement of each individual takes place. To the outsider it looks much like a circle of people standing and holding hands round an imaginary, communal circular hot bath sunk into the floor, and gingerly testing the temperature of the water first with one foot and then the other, all in rhythm with the music. Eventually, after endless bars of more shrills from the band, some sort of a crescendo is reached and the dancers become momentarily paroxysmal, perhaps on the collective decision to jump in, and that ends that particular *Sardana*. It may not be much of a spectacle but the enthusiasm of the participants shows it must be fun to do.

The mountain of Montserrat

That Montserrat – Montse for short – must surely be the most popular name for girls in Catalonia is an indication of how deeply entrenched is the Catalans' admiration for the patroness of the region, *la Mare de Déu de Montserrat*, popularly known as *La Moreneta*. The name Montserrat means 'saw-toothed mountain', which is as good a descriptive tag as any for this unusual geological feature which peaks at 1,245 metres – not *that* high – at the point where the sanctuary of *St Jeronimo* stands today. If one of Gaudí's clients, disregarding the question of his sanity for even contemplating such an idea, had ever commissioned him to design a mountain the result might well have looked something like this, a vast outcrop of rounded, smooth and sometimes phallic-shaped pinnacles of rock soaring up in layers to form a unique skyline, unlike any of the conventional shapes you would normally associate with a mountain. It was of course just such strange forms in nature that were often the inspiration behind his work.

The geological origins of Montserrat go back ten million years when this substantial crag somehow emerged from an inland sea. It is not volcanic, as is often believed, but is composed of conglomerate rocks, and the strange shapes are strictly the result of erosion and have encouraged generations of Catalan mountaineers to cut their teeth scaling some of the more difficult rock climbs here. Another feature of the mountain is its numerous caves, some of which have been illuminated and can be visited.

The basilica which houses the early-thirteenth-century statue of the diminutive *Moreneta*, so called because she is, in fact, black, is part of Benedictine community which has been on the mountain since 1027 when Abbott Oliba, a noted intellectual of his time, set up shop here. The original monastery buildings were destroyed by Napoleon's troops in 1811 so that what you see today is relatively recent.

No Catalan writer or poet with a reputation to maintain would risk not going on record with something profound about the spiritual significance which Montserrat and *La Moreneta* have for the Catalans: Joan Maragall, the nineteenth-century poet, was almost restrained when he called Montserrat 'something which belongs to us, resembling nothing else, it is completely outside the laws of nature', 'a gigantic castle with its tightly packed battlements' and claimed more forcefully, 'Montserrat is the Catalan miracle'. Jacint Verdaguer, a contemporary of Maragall and a poet/priest who went a long way in bringing a sense of Catalan nationalism back into vogue in the second half of the nineteenth century, was more lyrical with

Amb serra d'or els angelets serraren
eixos turons per fer-vos un palau.

With a golden saw the cherubs cut
These peaks to make you a palace.

But it was Josep Pla, the much-respected twentieth-century Catalan writer noted for his generally terse and usually very readable prose, who got really carried away interpreting the significance of *La Moreneta*:

(She is)...the brightest sparkle of the spirituality of a people who love La Moreneta and who are united with Montserrat not only by geographical ties but also through ancestral, consanguineous bonds, by a continuity, by a perpetuity.' This sounds as though it was written after a good lunch.

Montserrat is quite close to Barcelona, less than seventy kilometres by road, and offers a breathtaking drive up the side of the mountain to the monastery complex. Apart from the interest the rock formations hold as a spectacle there are cable car rides up almost vertical rock faces, the basilica and *La Moreneta* can be visited, and at mid-day the monastery's boy choir, *la escolania*, sings in the church. However you should be aware that this is one of the most popular day-excursions for tourists from all over Catalonia, two and a half million making the trip every year so you will have to compete with bus loads of people wanting to see the same things as you.

Club de Golf Terramar

Located just outside Sitges this club, the second oldest in Catalonia, was founded in 1922, and was originally built as a nine-hole course. Today's eighteen-hole layout measures 5,790 metres (6,332 yards) for a par of seventy two, with only five holes running over land on which the original course was built.

The player gets his first warning that the quality of maintenance on the course may not be up to the average for the region when he warms up on the practice tee, which is distinctly rough, and the quality of turf out on the fairways has, indeed, been patchy at best in recent years. The explanation usually given for this is that the water in Sitges is saline, which you will notice for example in the water in the showers, and that the grass out on the course suffers in consequence. If this is the reason one would expect the greens to be similarly below standard but they are in fact in good condition. All of this need not deter the golfer because the club allows you to clean and place your ball on the fairways all year round.

As at most seaside courses there is something special in the air at Terramar accentuated, perhaps, by the brighter light and the contrast of the greenness of the turf against the blue sea although only the first four and the last two holes actually run close to the shore. The first hole, which is the stroke index 1, is one of the most exacting first holes in the region, requiring a draw on the tee-shot to avoid bunkers and pine trees to the right and a storm drain and out-of-bounds to the left; the tee lines you up straight at the bunkers. The second shot to the green is also tight with the OB running all the way down the left hand side of the fairway and the green itself well protected by more bunkers. If the visitor comes out well on the first there is little to worry him until the eleventh, a 506 metre (553 yard) par five with a straightforward tee-shot followed by a second which has to be coaxed between water lying on both sides of the fairway right up to the green. The sixteenth, stroke index 2, is a good par four dog-leg which runs downhill to the green and invites you to cut the corner over the out-of-bounds to the left and so save some distance. The eighteenth is played right before the gallery sipping their beers out on the terrace under the flaming bougainvillea and the diners with a window seat in the restaurant, so fluffed shots are out!

The view from a seat on the terrace was one of the prettiest in Catalan golf with just the green strip of the eighteenth fairway and a line of single pines, bent by the wind, marking the foreground to the blue sea and sky beyond. This was before the municipal authorities planted a sewage pumping station right on the sea front, which would not matter if it had been decently hidden; instead two very noticeable metal cylinders inevitably attract your eye and spoil the view. Preserving natural beauty spots from the intrusions of the modern world is still not the priority it should be in a country whose biggest industry by far is tourism.

This club has an excellent restaurant so you might decide to lunch here with the Prince of the Putter after his round. The fixed menu is marvellous value for Ptas 1,300 (excluding wine and mineral water, and even fish would find the water that comes out of the tap salty), and if *calamarcitos a la plancha*, grilled baby squid, are on the menu they are as fresh and tender as you will find anywhere. A bottle of Conde de Caralt from the Penedès defends that D.O.'s colours in style and allows you to pay tribute to the local wine.

Sitges

The Garraf massif separates Sitges from Barcelona and establishes something of a climatic change too, the landscape south of the massif becoming drier looking without being truly arid. By road the distance is only thirty kilometres so if you preferred to make this pleasant little town your base in the Barcelona area the golfer can easily get to the courses around the big city from here.

Sitges has something of the atmosphere of a small coastal Andalusian town, full of narrow streets with whitewashed houses and small sunny squares. Only Tossa de Mar on the Costa Brava shares this southern character, almost out-of-keeping with the rest of Catalonia, but both do have the charm that only small intimate townships seem to enjoy. Sitges also has one of the finest seaside promenades in the region, stretching two and a half kilometres southwards from what has become virtually the town's logo, the parish church of *Sant Bartolomé* and *Santa Tecla*.

A lot of people live year round in Sitges and commute to the big city and many others have weekend homes here so that in the summer months this place is buzzing, and its narrow beaches are as tightly packed as the last U.S. helicopter out of Saigon; it also has a quite large gay community who are more in evidence in the summer.

Until the end of the nineteenth century Sitges was little more than a quiet backwater, home to fishermen, a few stevedores, who worked on the loading of vessels exporting wine from the Penedès to the American colonies, and those employed in the vineyards. Then in 1871 one of those Catalans who had emigrated to the Americas to make their fortunes prior to returning home to enjoy their riches, Francesc Gumà i Ferran, an *Indiano* as these successful ex-colonists were called, arrived in the neighbouring town of Vilanova determined to make a mark for himself in local society: he would bring the railway from Barcelona along the coast to Vilanova. The first train inaugurated the line in 1881, and from then on Sitges and Vilanova were on the map.

An early beneficiary of the ease of access to Sitges from Barcelona via the railway was Santiago Rusiñol, one of the founder members of the 'Quatre Gats' café in Barcelona. Born in 1861 and the son of a wealthy textile magnate, Rusiñol had enough financial security through his family to be able to indulge the life of a fashionable, well-heeled bohemian artist, who spent some years immersed in the vibrant fin-de-siècle art world in Paris before returning to Barcelona where, together with his friend and fellow artist, Ramón Casas, he was a prime mover in Modernisme as it affected art. He was also a writer of some repute although he preferred to be considered an artist, and one of his satirical tales, *L'Auca de Senyor Esteve* (The story of Sr Esteve) is still performed in theatres today. In 1891, when he was thirty one and already a name in Barcelona intellectual circles, Rusiñol paid a visit to Vilanova and decided to spend the night in the adjacent fishing village of Sitges and immediately fell in love with the place. As he later recounted, 'I, my friends, was wandering around the world, working the terrain, leaping up and down dale, when one day I saw a place that was sunnier than other places, the sky was bluer and so was the sea, the houses were white but not from the snow, everything was green and in flower, and here I stayed.'

He purchased a property perched right over the sea and made it his studio, home and a cultural centre as well where, amidst items representative of Modernisme as manifested in painting, music, theatre and poetry he put his large collection of forged iron-work, which for him represented the essence of pure rural Catalan art, 'an art without aesthetic rules ... an art as free as smoke'. He called the house Cau Ferrat, the iron den, and left it to the town in his will so that today, now a museum and still called Cau Ferrat, you can visit it and all that he had put inside.

Rusiñol loved to play the flamboyant eccentric artist in public and would make the most of any opportunity to do so. His annual 'Moderniste festivals', which he organized in Sitges between 1892 to 1899, were soon so popular that special trains were arranged from Barcelona to bring those wishing to experience the high jinks, and they were not usually disappointed. In the 1894 *festa moderniste* the highlight event was a ritual delivery of two El Greco paintings he had earlier acquired in Paris to Cau Ferrat. A train with over sixty guests arrived from Barcelona with the two paintings, which were met at the station by a brass band, the writer Narcis Oller, the architect Puig i Cadalfalch, Joan Maragall, the poet, and Rusiñol's artist friend Ramón Casas. The paintings were ceremoniously born on high through the crowd at the funeral pace of an Easter week procession. Maragall was later to refer to the event as one of 'slightly childish snobbery' and although most of the participants did not really think much of the two strange paintings 'we all believed in modernisme'. The paintings, '*The tears of St. Peter*' and '*The penitent Santa Magdalena*' are still on view in the museum together with paintings by Rusiñol himself, Ramón Casas, Utrillo and Zuluaga.

Rusiñol's Moderniste festivals established Sitges as a place that would henceforth host events that cultivated the theatrical side of life. Today the Sitges Carnival is the most exotic in the region, and the town also hosts an annual Horror Movie festival. There are other interesting museums in Sitges and Vilanova where you can see how life was lived in a typical house between the eighteenth and nineteenth centuries (Casa Llopis in Sitges), the *Museu Romàntic* (Can Papiol in Vilanova) and nineteenth- and twentieth-century Catalan art in the *Museu Victor Balaguer* in Vilanova.

It is always a pleasure to be in Sitges.

~ VIII ~

The District of El Maresme

Club de Golf Llavaneres

El Maresme is the name given to the stretch of coast which runs north from Barcelona to the estuary of the river Tordera just below Blanes. It is a narrow strip of land formed by a line of hills rising to around four hundred metres, some six kilometres back from the coast. Even a euphoric drunk would not describe the beaches, blighted by a busy main road and railway line running right along the edge of the sea, as beautiful but the 45-kilometre riviera of El Maresme is considered a choice residential area close to the big city. Houses built in and around the little villages, all of which have millenary histories and populate the seaward slopes of the hills, look out over the coastline which is far enough away for its less attractive features to be hidden while emphasising the fact that the sea is really quite close. The beaches, even if not tourist brochure pretty, are still very handy for the local residents in the summer months and the micro-climate with its 270 days of sunshine per year is, as everyone will make a point of telling you, especially benign with tolerably cool nights in the summer and balmy sunny days in the winter months when you can sit outside the bars and enjoy your mid-day aperitivo provided the Levante is not blowing. The winter nights are fresh enough for you to enjoy a fire in the evenings but the temperature rarely falls below six degrees or so centigrade, and if it does everyone begins to complain bitterly about the severity of the winter.

The village of Sant Andreu de Llavaneres lies thirty five kilometres north of Barcelona, almost midway along El Maresme and just three kilometres inland. El Club de Golf Llavaneres is right below the village and as you walk along the veranda and terrace in front of the clubhouse the views out over the coast towards Mataró to the south and Arenys de Mar to the north are such that regardless of your normal indifference to the game of golf and the relative intricacies of a given golf course you might even envy the golfer's pleasure at playing in a scenario as visually intoxicating as this. But then again you might already have decided that if golf spoils a good walk it may well also blind the addicts who play it to the splendours of the scenery. As usual, you are probably right.

This is an intimate family-style golf club, founded in 1945 by the residents of weekend homes in the area who wanted to indulge their preferred pastime near to their residence at a time when there were only three other courses in Catalonia. Originally a nine-hole course it was enlarged to eighteen holes in 1990 and it still retains something of a family atmosphere. The old clubhouse has recently been enlarged but the members have sensibly retained the cosier corners, including the fireplace of the original building which, with its well-worn leather sofas, has the patina of an old but comfortable classic. The course is short at 4,644 metres (5,079 yards) for a par of sixty eight and apart from a long par five of 507 metres (554 yards) with an uphill tee-shot, and a view from the seventeenth tee way down to a green backed by palm tees, a shimmering sea and the sky, which puts it among the most handsome of golfing vistas in Catalonia, no other feature on the course stands out in golfing terms. It is the perfect course for enjoying a gentle relaxed round of golf. It is also a course which will attract anyone who appreciates playing in beautiful surroundings because here, apart from the views out over the coast, much care has been taken over the years to fill the course with a variety of trees and shrubs that would not look out of place in an amateur botanist's private park. Orange trees line the first fairway and from there on you play surrounded by a decorative display of trees and bushes, many of them flowering varieties and so in bloom in the spring and early summer.

Back in the clubhouse after your local excursion and waiting for the fourteen-wand magician to join you after his round you can relax on that seductive veranda, sunk deep into a well padded wicker armchair with the sun soaking into you even in January at mid-day, and drink in the view while he is enjoying a shower in the new ritzy changing rooms with their elegant polished teak floor. When he emerges a glass or two of Signat *cava* would be a fitting tribute to the visual feast laid out below you and stretching far out over the unfailingly blue Mediterranean sea.

Alella and Signat *cava*

The village of Alella, just inland from El Masnou and its attractive yacht marina on the Maresme coast, is one of the recognized quality wine-growing areas in Catalonia with its own D.O. – *Denominación de Origen*. The area in which grapes are grown for Alella wine is quite small, 350 hectares, so production is limited but it has a long and well-established reputation for fine white wines, most of which are produced by the village wine cooperative. The Romans stored wine in the neighbouring village of Tiana but it was in the nineteenth century that Alella wine acquired its reputation and Alella Marfil, its best known brand, became the fashionable wine to drink in the music halls of Barcelona as well as at society dinners. It was exported to the colonies, a nostalgic reminder of the fatherland for the *Indianos*, as the expatriate Catalans who had emigrated to the 'Indies' were called by their fellow countrymen and who often suffered from *enyorança* – homesickness. The characteristics of Alella wine result from the two subtly different areas in which the vines grow: some on the seaward slopes of the hills, growing in very porous granity soil and exposed to the sun and sea breezes all day long giving the wine a fine balance between alcohol content and rather light acidity; the others, grown to the west of the coastal hills, receiving less sun have a lower alcohol content and are more acid. The blend of the two makes a full bodied, mildly fruity wine.

The impression the *Indianos* made on nineteenth-century Catalan society was far superior to their numbers. In part this was a case of the old established bourgeoisie despising the new rich but more often it was flagrant envy of those who had risked everything, including their lives in the perilous sea voyages there and back when a fatal illness could kill you even if the storms did not, and who could now lead the life of the very wealthy. Opportunities for getting a good job in Catalonia were normally few and for actually improving one's position in society virtually zero so a quite widely held tenet of what to do with the next generation once it was out of childhood was '*Les noies, a servir. Els nois a America*' – 'The girls into service. The boys to America'. Tales of returning sailors and soldiers augmented the perception that with a bit of hard graft and sacrifice an able-bodied man could indeed make his fortune in the colonies. In practice only a small number did but such was the impact of their lifestyles on their return that the general impression was one of hundreds rather than tens of successful *Indianos*.

Most invested their money in land and property, a few bought businesses or put their money into the stock exchange, and the question of making a good marriage to protect the hard-earned fortune was primal, so much so that several married nieces to ensure that the money would stay in the family.

When David Coll decided to start his own *cava* business he looked for a property which would give the right cachet to a product that depends as much on prestige as on quality, and when he came across an abandoned and quite derelict old house in Alella built in the previous century by an *Indiano* he knew he had found just what he needed. A substantial chunk of money and a few grey hairs later the cellars and distinguished headquarters for his exclusive *cava* were in place. His philosophy from the start was to spare no effort and cut no corners in pursuing only the highest quality in every step of the process of producing a fine *cava*. Signat, as his *cava* is called, is produced only in small quantities but the quality is superb. If you visit his *celler* in Alella, and visitors are welcomed with great hospitality, you will quickly see that this business is a labour of love and Signat the chosen child. All this may sound too good to be true but the *cava* professionals do not think so: in the 1998 edition of the Spanish wine trade yearbook Signat scored the highest of all the *cavas* in Spain.

There are several good restaurants on the Maresme ranging from a Michelin two-star establishment in Sant Pol de Mar down through different price and quality levels to simple places with good value, fixed menus. The marina at El Masnou has the greatest concentration of establishments in one place but for value for money in unpretentious surroundings 'El Bar del Puerto' in Arenys de Mar is difficult to beat provided you are a fish eater. This is a simple little place run by a family who over the years have refined the list of dishes on offer to what the majority of customers seem to enjoy most, all at reasonable prices, so that it has become an enormously popular venue. The cooking is based on the grill and the fish, bought at the daily fish auction in the port, is day-fresh. At the weekends and on any day in the summer months you need to get in early to avoid having to queue. A walk round this attractive port with a sizable fishing fleet and the best maintained marina between Barcelona and France will add to your enjoyment of the meal.

~ IX ~

Tarragona

Introduction to Tarragona

To get in a suitably historical frame of mind for your visit to the capital of Catalonia's southernmost province you should exit the A-7 motorway at El Vendrell and head south on the N-340. You are now on the Via Augusta, the Romans' highway connecting Spain with Rome, and within a few kilometres the road bisects round a triumphal arch, *el Arc de Berà*, built in the first century AD in compliance with a request made in his will by the Emperor Trajan's consul in Tarraco, as Tarragona was called by the Romans. It is still in excellent condition, an impressive piece of Roman monumental architecture which heralds your approach to what was their capital in the northern province of the Iberian peninsula, Hispania Citerior.

Before the Romans arrived Phoenicians and, later, Greeks had settlements here – it was *Caliópolis*, 'the beautiful city' to the Greeks. Hannibal also had a military base here to protect his lines of supply to Carthage but it was two Roman brothers, Publius and Cnaeus Scipio who, around 218 BC, founded what was to be a major Roman city. Just why they chose this point on the coast is not known but almost certainly there was an existing Ibero settlement on which they could base the future city. What was to make it so important was its port, which was the entry point for everything coming from Rome to the colony, and it grew into a substantial town over the next four hundred years. By the second century AD the population was over thirty thousand and the city had all the major buildings that were to be found in the big urban centres in the empire – defensive walls, temples, palaces, a Forum, circus and amphi-theatre for gladiatorial contests and chariot racing, and the remains of these can all be seen today. Building in modern Tarragona, in addition to all the usual logistical problems of erecting a new structure in a busy town, has to cater for the requirements of the archaeologists who need to analyze and plot the wealth of historical debris that emerges whenever

158

excavations for the foundations of a new building are dug, and this is a town where not only the Romans left ample evidence of their time here but also succeeding inhabitants – Visigoths, Saracens, and then generations of Catalans from the eleventh century to the present day.

Under the Romans Tarraco's most splendid era was probably around the second century AD although much earlier it had been the military base for such historical giants as Julius Caesar and the first Roman Emperor, Augustus, who was Caesar's nephew, adopted son and eventual successor. For whatever reason, it was Augustus who left an indelible imprint on Catalonia with the Via Augusta, one of Barcelona's main arteries, an everyday reminder of his presence here to the modern Barcelonese.

Club de Golf Costa Dorada Tarragona

Located on rising ground a few kilometres inland and only a fifteen-minute drive from the provincial capital of Tarragona the Club de Golf Costa Dorada Tarragona enjoys an epicurean climate winter and summer. While the heat makes it preferable to play after four in the afternoon in the summer months when a sea breeze gets up and fans the players, it is one of the Costa Dorada's climatic blessings to tee-off at, say, ten on a January morning and by noon to have slipped out of the light sweater you started in and enjoy the rest of the round in warm spring-like weather. No wonder that the Romans made Tarraco – Tarragona – their capital in the northern half of Spain.

To reach the course from Tarragona leave the city on the N-340 coast road heading north and just ten minutes' drive will bring you to the turn-off at Moinàs for Catllar. Drive inland through vineyards until you see the signpost for the golf club which is only about five minutes further on.

The dazzling luminosity, a feature of the southern part of Catalonia, strikes you as you drive in through a plantation of miniature palm trees and then up to the bougainvillea-ed walls of the clubhouse which looks like a large masia and so in keeping with the surroundings, and you might as well stay for a coffee in the bar where the friendliness of the staff is typical of everyone you deal with at this club, before leaving the professor with a doctorate in golf to his duties. He faces a 5,978 metre (6,538 yard), par seventy two delightfully varied layout which is not physically taxing.

The view from the clubhouse, which sits on the highest part of the course, is out over pine trees and vineyards with the Mediterranean clear on the south-eastern horizon, a thin strip of deep blue separating the pale sky from the green cover of the land but with Tarragona itself hidden from your view.

The professor will find the practice tee rather small and cramped compared to others in the region but this is in no way mirrored on the course itself, a layout with average width fairways and greens in proportion, which was built on land cultivated as vineyards and olive groves, and some holes are still dotted with olive trees.

He will tee-off on the first, a 511 metre (559 yard) downward sloping par five, with a few olive trees standing on the sides of the fairway, in the direction of the sea and should find the green in easy range of his third shot. Looking back up the fairway from the green you can see the different levels, which were previously terraced vineyards, defined by beautifully constructed stone walls sensibly left in place by the designer, José Gancedo, and neat examples of the skills required in dry-stonewalling. Terracing of the land was a feature of Mediterranean cultivation but it is incompatible with the mechanized farming of the modern world.

On the third hole the tee-shot must be kept on the left of the fairway otherwise it will slip into some bunkers on the right, which are invisible from the tee, or into the rough if he really loses it to the right. After the short par three fourth comes a 335 metre (366 yard) dog-leg where the tee-shot needs to be put in the centre-right of the fairway to open up the elevated green. A couple of pines in the fairway add an inconvenience, of questionable justification from a design standpoint, to the drive. By now your golfer should be aware of and enjoying the variety of trees and shrubs planted around the course which add a lot to its visual appeal.

The second nine holes have a different character to the first being rather more open and give the player opportunities to recover shots lost on the first nine. The thirteenth, rated the stroke index 1 hole, is the longest par five in Catalonia at 560 metres (612 yards) and if he makes it to the green with his third he can be excused for feeling rather macho because, among other reasons, he managed to play his fairway wood on the second shot over some pines in the fairway left just where they can do most harm. The next hole is a demanding par four, uphill to the green from the fall of the drive with the second shot required to clear what amounts to an olive grove left in the fairway on the last 150 metres to the green.

The sixteenth is a tough par five with a lake to catch the drive if he slices it and which he has to cross with his second. By the time he prepares to play his third to the green his patience with the designer will probably have run out because once again tall pines have been left standing, making a conventional approach to the green impossible. Sensible golf courses, even very challenging ones, should be designed for the handicap golfer, the typical club member, to play and leaving trees standing which intentionally penalize a well-struck shot by the golfer of average ability is like spitting in your eye. The mid-handicap player has enough of a problem just repeating his swing in a more or less consistent fashion without facing obstacles like trees in the fairway right in the line of a shot.

The last two holes are straightforward so by the time he gets back to the clubhouse he should, once again, be back in an amiable mood and over his irritation with all those trees blocking the fairways, and a cool beer will quickly restore him to his usual, serene self. If it doesn't, invite him to a second.

X X X

Roman Tarragona

This is another town where you can do almost all of your sightseeing on foot, and a good place to start is the Roman amphitheatre built almost on the beach below the centre of the town. What remains of it reveals an elliptical theatre with terraced seating all around the arena where gladiators did their gory duty before the assembled citizens. Regrettably most of what you see today are reconstructions of the original Roman edifice except where the terraced seating was actually cut into the basaltic rock around the arena, which presumably was done by the Romans; everything else is a rubble and cement outline of the original. At the southern end of the arena the original Roman entrance is still standing, however, and gives you a fair idea of how the rest must have looked, and the overall shape and proportions of the amphitheatre are clearly those of the original. Down in the arena are the remains of two early Christian churches, one from the time of the Visigoths, one of whose kings, Recaredo, converted to Christianity, and the other from the twelfth century.

Overlooking the amphitheatre stands the *Pretori de Pilats*, the Praetorium or Roman governor's residence, and also called *el Castell del Rei* (the King's Castle) and *el Palau August* (Augustus' Palace). This tall, unembellished but beautiful stone fortress-like structure, today part of the city's historical museum, is a prime example of how succeeding generations have adapted and used buildings constructed as much as two thousand years ago to each era's needs. The Romans used it as an administrative centre for the province; the Catalan-Aragonese monarchs rebuilt it and used it as a palace when they were in residence in the city, and it has a long history as a detention centre from the year 239 when the first Tarragonese martyrs, bishop Fructuós and his deacons Auguri and Eulogi, were imprisoned here, until as recently as the 1950s under the Franco regime. Under this building you can visit remains of the Roman circus, a large arena used primarily for chariot racing and other equestrian events.

The Roman Forum is located at some distance from the other interesting sites in the city but you can take a breather from the purely historical if you plan your route there via the Rambla Nova, a handsome central street on which the pedestrians are allotted more space than the traffic by means of a wide, tree-lined pedestrian walkway down the middle. At the top end is a the *Balcò de la Mediterrani*, a paved terrace which provides a good viewing point out over the port and amphitheatre. If the sun is out a coffee at one of the café tables on the Rambla will give your feet a rest and your eyes the opportunity to absorb the tourists and the locals as they drift past you.

If a meal is your immediate priority the restaurant 'La Rambla' close to the Balcò on the Rambla Nova has a *suquet de raya amb gambas i cloïssos*, a fish stew of skate with prawns, clams and potatoes which you will probably put near the top of your list of favourite Catalan dishes. If you choose the house red to have with your meal it turns out to be a wine from the D.O. Tarragona, a young, fruity pleasant wine which unless you specify otherwise will be served chilled, an experience to be tried at least once because it does add something to the character of a young red wine. For your dessert you should try a *Crema catalana* which is possibly the most celebrated of all Catalan desserts and is similar to a light custard topped with caramel. There are other little restaurants full of character in the *casc antic*, the old quarter around the cathedral: two such are 'El Rebost' (The Cellar) on the *carrer de la Nau*, and 'Restaurant Merlot' on the *carrer dels Cavallers*.

With your batteries recharged the Forum awaits you, a place of significance in a Roman town, and this one occupied an area of 42,000 square metres. What can be seen here are some of the columns which supported the roof over a Portico surrounding the main area, part of a paved street and outlines of Roman houses.

What the city tourist office calls *El Passeig Arquelògic*, the archaeological promenade, is a walkway round part of the formidable Roman walls built at the beginning of the second century BC. These were originally four kilometres long but today only one kilometre is still standing with three substantial towers spaced out along it. It is a thoroughly impressive piece of defensive engineering, twelve metres high and between four and six metres thick. An unusual feature of the wall, and a surprise to archaeologists, is its base made up of large uncut rocks, some as big as four metres long by three metres wide and each weighing up to three and a half tons. Above this the rest of the wall is ashlar stone still in fine condition after 2,200 years. Such was the effectiveness of the wall that down the centuries it was never breached, the only successful attacks on the town being those which were launched from the sea. Succeeding generations have adopted parts of the wall as part of their buildings so that today, in places, there are windows built into the wall providing light to some dwelling behind it. There are fine views out over the Tarragona countryside from the *passeig*, which can be best enjoyed in the late afternoon when the western sun highlights the stone. Inside the town the walls are just part of the city scenery, today's traffic sliding through the original gates just as horse-drawn carts and chariots did two millennia ago.

The masterpiece of Roman engineering in Tarragona is the aqueduct, popularly known as *el Pont del Diable*, the Devil's Bridge, located just outside the city but easy to visit because the A-7 motorway runs right by it and there is a viewing area to park in. Two things stand out when you look at the aqueduct: it shows, first, that the Romans were very competent engineers, capable of designing free-standing, aesthetically pleasing, masonry structures in uncompromising terrain; secondly, such was the quality of their stone masonry that its condition today has the appearance of a structure built no more than two hundred years ago. Just like the Roman aqueduct in Segovia it is a handsome example of their engineering abilities.

The Archaeological Museum has a wealth of items of all types from the early Greeks to the Iberos, Romans and Visigoths, a wonderful collection of over 25,000 objects including Roman sarcophagi, friezes, capitals, amphoras, unguentaries, figurines, diverse glass objects, statues and treasure chests.

Aigüesverds Club de Golf

The town of Reus, the birthplace of Antoni Gaudí, is just a few kilometres south and west of Tarragona, and the Aigüesverds (*Green Waters*) Golf Club is on the outskirts of the town right in the hazelnut and almond growing area of Catalonia. To be precise we are in the district of the Baix Camp but to the occasional visitor there is nothing in the terrain nor the vegetation to distinguish it from the district around Tarragona, the Tarragonès. They share the same intense light and a countryside of predominantly white calcareous rocks and stones lying on ochre-coloured earth liberally populated with vines and olive and pine trees. It is is noticeably drier than the province of Girona but without deserving the label of arid.

The entrance driveway into the club is impressive, a palm tree-ed induction into a place which is going to offer more glamour than golf, you could be forgiven for thinking but, once parked, the white club-house, built in a classical Mediterranean style, tones in decently with the surroundings and turns out to be hardly visible from the golf course. Inside, it is sized sensibly for the functions it has to house, leaving you with a feeling of comfort without large areas of superfluous space.

The course itself, at 5,937 metres (6,151 yards) from the yellow tees for a par of seventy two, is almost flat but manages to offer plenty of variety. The first is a tame par four and will set your man up nicely for the second, which requires a drive over water to a fairway lined with eucalyptus and pines with the Sierra de Montsant forming a hazy and distant horizon behind the green. The par three third has a an island green but at only 122 metres (133 yards) should not worry anyone even if this is a novel golfing experience.

The long par five fourth has a generously wide fairway as do all the holes on this course and, after two woods, leaves an uphill third to a sharply-sloping green. The fifth is the stroke index 1 hole, more for the dangers of going out-of-bounds on the drive – possible to the left, to the right and straight down the track if you hit it too far – than for any other intrinsic difficulty. By this time in his day the golfer should be able to distinguish an almond from a hazelnut tree because he will have seen plenty of both since he started although as the course unfolds he will see a good variety of other trees as well.

A huge bunker some 215 metres (235 yards) from the tee and invisible from it fills three quarters of the width of the eighth fairway but otherwise this hole presents no problems. The ninth, a par four, plays to a tight green protected by an ornamental lake complete with ducks so the shot to the green is over water. The fairway on this hole is bordered by large oleanders giving a splash of colour all through the summer when most other flowering plants are wilting in the heat.

The second nine holes are perhaps a little less varied than the first nine, with olive trees and the occasional *algarroba* (carob tree) much in evidence. The fifteenth is a long and challenging par five and the last hole, a friendly short par four, has two tall slim cypress trees behind the green closing off the clubhouse from the golfer's view as he tees-off and providing a touch of style to stay in his memory as he ends his round and contemplates that long cool lager waiting for him in the clubhouse.

Quality is the term which best summarizes this golf course which certainly cannot be described as over difficult, and although there are days when the wind blows quite strongly the local climate is otherwise benign year round. Before leaving, make a point of viewing the beautifully staged Haitian swimming pool located near the entrance to the clubhouse but hidden behind trees; there is not, as yet, another one like it in Catalunya.

X X X

The cathedral
The cathedral of *Santa Tecla* stands on the highest part of the city and is believed to be on the same site as the Roman temple of Jupiter and a later Arab mosque. Its initiator was archbishop Hugh de Cervelló, who died in 1171 and left his cash for the construction of a cathedral. Work began in 1174 and it was consecrated in 1350, fully 176 years later, not an unreasonable period of time for such a monumental undertaking but nevertheless illustrative of the kind of unwavering commitment clerics had to their building programmes given the political uncertainty of the times; who today would put in place a programme whose final outcome will be two generations on?

Considered to be the most beautiful example in Spain of a church built in the transitionary period between Romanesque and Gothic, its warm ochre-tinged stone reflects the brilliant light of southern Catalunya as it stands high above the mediaeval quarter of the city. At the entrance to the cathedral complex the visitor is given the best guide to any major historical building in the region, a very practical and detailed leaflet detailing all of the major contents in the cathedral and the diocesan museum, each identified by numbers which are repeated on the objects themselves. It is such a good system that one wonders why other historical sites do not adopt it in Tarragona and elsewhere.

The guide gives you a recommended route to follow for your visit to the cathedral, cloister and the museum. The large cloister is one of the most beautiful in Catalonia and combines details from the early Gothic period, Romanesque carved figurines and Moorish ornamentation in the semicircular arches. Once inside the cathedral proper there is such a wealth of glorious detail that you will quickly realize that, to do it justice, you will need time. There are thirty side chapels, each rich in detail, and what must be the largest collection of seventeenth-century Brussels tapestries outside Belgium, twenty two in total, hung in different parts of the nave and side chapels. The rose window in the main façade is one of the largest in Europe and opposite it, at the other end of the central nave, is the magnificent altar-piece of the main altar carved in alabaster by a renowned craftsman of the fifteenth century, Pere Joan, who was also responsible for the altar-piece in the cathedral in Zaragoza. The choir, formed by Gothic carved wooden seating and the splendid Renaissance organ, carved by Jerónimo Sancho and Pere Ostrin, set off the high altar, illuminated by an octagonal cupola rising ten metres above the roof of the nave. As a whole it is much richer in decoration and style than the cathedrals in Girona and Barcelona.

El casc antic, the old quarter
The old quarter in Tarragona is another invitation just to stroll through mediaeval streets and enjoy the shops, old doorways and the general atmosphere. Starting from the cathedral you can follow a route which will allow you to see the stylish façade of the old hospital of *Santa Tecla*, built between the twelfth and fourteenth centuries, then several Gothic arches which lead on to the old Jewish quarter, and finish up at the *Museo Nacional Arqueològic*. No great distance is involved and just how long you spend wandering round will depend on your enjoyment of this historical milieu.

Club de Golf Residencial Bonmont Terres Noves
The course at this club whose official name must have been decided by a committee but has since been abbreviated by the golfing world to 'Bonmont', is a Robert Trent Jones Jr design, and at 6,050 metres (6,616

yards) for a par of seventy two, is a serious challenge for the golfer's skills and, unquestionably, a layout of high quality overlooking the coast some thirty kilometres south of Tarragona. Like most Trent Jones designs it is heavily bunkered, more than ninety traps making it second in the region after Fontanals in La Cerdanya in this respect which, together with the difficulty here of the rocky ravines bordering many of the fairways and very much a feature of this layout, means accuracy is essential for a good result. Most holes have quite generous fairways but as the area at the fall of the tee-shot is usually bunkered on both sides wayward drives are almost always penalized. Putting on the undulating greens is not easy and many of the greens are difficult to read. If the golfer's visit to Bonmont happens to coincide with a day when the Mestral is whistling down from the sierra behind the course he will feel a hero if he lasts the eighteen holes and a lucky one, too, if he is still united with his hat at the end of his round.

As you drive through the security control at the entrance to the luxury residential complex in which the course is located, and up past some of the substantial residences the quality of detail everywhere is an indication of what is to be found on the course itself. And the standard is high: virtually unblemished tees, excellent turf on the fairways, rough which is kept sensibly short, greens in excellent condition winter and summer, and sand in the bunkers worthy of a course that has hosted two 'Opens de Catalunya' in the last seven years.

The first hole is a friendly par five of 458 metres (501 yards) on which a lake has to be negotiated but not crossed on the second shot, just the kind of hole that allows the player to start his day with a par to boost his confidence. The short par four second looks another easy par from the tee with the fairway sloping down to the green. However, the rock-strewn ravine running all the way down the left of the fairway and then across the front of the green plus the bunkers guarding the right of the fairway can cause untold havoc on the uninitiated, and it is not unusual for the first-time visitor to miss the par opportunity offered. The 150 metre (164 yard) par three fifth requires dropping the tee-shot on the putting surface to avoid finishing in the ravine stretching from the tee right to the edge of the green. Another hidden ravine will also swallow up anything right of the fairway on the second shot to the green on the stroke index 2, sixth hole, and the tee-shot on the par three eighth has to be just right to hold the shallow green and avoid the lake running alongside it.

The second nine are appreciably harder than the outward half. From the twelfth to the sixteenth each hole, which includes two long par fours, plays unremittingly uphill, making these holes play longer than their real metreage. The seventeenth is the signature hole, a par five running downhill bordered by trouble on both sides and reachable in two by the longer hitters if they risk using the driver off the tee but they will need a calm pulse and the serenity of mind of a trapeze artist to play the second over another gaping ravine ending right at the edge of the green.

Back in the stylish clubhouse you can admire the view out over this part of the Costa Daurada which makes a splendid background to the course and residential area below you. If the golfer is feeling peckish you could order him a *bocadillo de jamón*, which will keep him busy for the next twenty minutes or so as he bites his way down to the other end of its half-metre length. They don't do things by halves at Bonmont.

Ⅹ Ⅹ Ⅹ

The monasteries of Poblet and Santes Creus

Within an hour's drive from Tarragona there are two great monasteries to visit, one of which, Poblet, still has a community of monks while Santes Creus is no longer occupied. Both were built by the Cistercian order, a no frills no home comforts version of the Benedictines, and both are impressively massive.

Santa Maria de Poblet in the district of Conca de Barberà is the largest Cistercian house in Europe, and was founded by twelve French monks in the twelfth century after the Catalan monarch, Ramón Berenguer IV, persuaded the abbot of Fontfreda in the French Languedoc region to build a similar establishment in the southern part of Catalonia, recently reconquered from the Moors. A generous gift of land from the king, enlarged by additional donations of acreage from the local nobility, was evidently sufficient inducement for the asset-conscious prelate to agree.

The clergy were the educated élite at the time and the Cistercians were, furthermore, rigorous observers of the rule of St Benet, based on the precept of *laborare est orare*, work is prayer, so the king saw in them the ideal formula for reintroducing Christianity into the area as well as giving agriculture a kick-start, the 'work' part of the ideal. Once the original buildings were finished the French returned to Fontfreda and left local monks who had joined the order to develop the business, as it were. And they did so very successfully, building farmhouses, called *granges* in this part of the region, each with its own chapel. The local peasant farmers were quick to occupy them and agriculture soon flourished, based on grain crops, olives, grapes for wine and fruit trees. These are still the backbone of agricultural production today. Meanwhile the monks were busy cultivating their own land, selling the crops for cash, which provided funding over the centuries for further building. By the eighteenth century the monastery had become a very wealthy establishment and one of the largest landowners in the region with properties stretching from the Pyrenees to Valencia.

From its beginnings Poblet was a pivotal institution in Catalan life. Apart from its agricultural enterprise the monastery was an important centre of learning: monks from Poblet were university professors in several European universities and others were sent abroad to further their studies, while those who stayed in Poblet combined intellectual tasks, such as documenting current events in the life of the monastery as well as others of historical importance in the kingdom, with the administration of the house's landed interests. It was usual for the reigning monarch to spend some time in residence in Poblet attending to affairs of state and consulting with the abbot on anything he considered would benefit from the disinterested opinion of an intellectual. No fewer than fourteen royal personages, either monarchs or their wives, were buried here, all between 1196 and 1479. From the royal perspective this was the place to lay your bones, in part as insurance of a passport to heaven and but also as a guarantee that your place in history would not be forgotten, your tomb an object of veneration by future generations in this most suitable pantheon for a king.

By the end of the fifteenth century Poblet was still a major player in Catalonia's institutional life: abbot Joan Payo Coello even became president of the *Generalitat* for three years during the reign of the Catholic Monarchs, an achievement to be repeated a century later by abbot Francesc Oliver de Boteller. In 1585 Philip II took part in an Easter week procession at the monastery but by the time of his death his own monastic creation, the Escorial, was finished and he and succeeding Spanish kings were to be buried there.

In the next three centuries, with the Ship of State firmly anchored in Madrid, the monastery went about its business while staying out of the mainstream of public life but it was still a respected centre of reference in regional affairs. Then in 1836-7 came that cataclysmic event for the

Church, the Mendizábal laws, which secularized church property. Thus one political decision stripped Poblet of all its properties, forever, and ended the community's life there. Coincidental with the State's expropriation policy, social upheaval produced a series of violent mob sackings of the monastery buildings, many of which were partly destroyed, apparently motivated by the erroneous belief that they held untold quantities of gold and precious stones; even the royal tombs were ripped open in the expectation of finding valuable jewellery inside them. The consequence of all this was the end of monastic life at Poblet until the twentieth century.

Gaudí was an ardent admirer of Poblet, which as a young man symbolized for him the the essence of Catalonia, a monument from the country's independent past and therefore something which cried out for restoration. He and a friend, Eduardo Toda, wrote the *Poblet Manuscript* describing the state of decay of the buildings and arguing the case for their restoration but it was after Gaudí's death that the first organization, the *Patronat de Poblet*, was formed in 1930, and it was only after the Spanish Civil War that restoration work began, and it has taken over forty years to complete. The result is magnificent and life, including a Cistercian community whose first members actually took up residence in the decade after the civil war, has returned to these imposing buildings.

What strikes the visitor first is the sheer size of the monastery and its outer defensive walls, giving it the look more of a fortified citadel than a religious house. Once inside the variety of architectural styles, ranging from the Romanesque to Gothic and, finally, Renaissance makes it a rich assemblage of historic buildings. Some of the present day community's living quarters are closed to the public but there are many buildings, including cloisters, chapels, the main church with its alabaster, Renaissance altar-piece, the library, the cellar and dormitory that are open to the public. It is worth checking in advance the times of guided tours to get the most out of your visit.

Santes Creus

Although not as large as Poblet this monastic institution in the district of the Alt Camp and lying between Poblet and Vilafranca del Penedès is still on the grand scale. As you approach it from the direction of Vilarodona you see it across a small valley, facing south and tinged with a warm golden glow in a late afternoon sun, its buildings escalating up sloping ground from the houses that form the village, a three-dimensional cubist-like composition of façades, rooftops, crenelated walls, domes and towers. Over the centuries this was clearly a massive undertaking.

It was in 1158 that that the Cistercian monks of the monastery of Valldaura del Valles were given some land on the rising banks of the Gaià river by two Catalan nobles, Montagut and de Albà. As in the case of Poblet this was territory recently taken from the Saracens and it needed redeveloping. As required by the code laid down by the founder of the order, St Bernard, a Cistercian house should be sited on land isolated from the affairs of man but with an abundance of water, and this lost corner of Catalonia fitted the bill perfectly. By 1174 the core of the monastery, the church, chapter house, lavabo and cloister were all under construction. A century later Abbot Gener obtained the patronage of the king, Pere el Gran, which brought with it additional funds to expand the building programme, and twenty five years later the Abbot's quarters were made a royal residence for Jaume II and his wife, Blanca de Anjou. In succeeding centuries the monastery continued to court kings, build, extend its ownership of land and its right to oversee other religious institutions as far as Rosellon in France; it was virtually the pattern twentieth-century multinationals would follow to grow their international business interests: grow or die. At the height of its prosperity the monastery sustained 220 people, of whom seventy seven were monks. Even men dedicated to God can, it seems, be subject to domestic spats and it needed a decision by Rome in 1751 to decide one between Santes Creus and Poblet as to which had precedence in certain matters, the umpire's decision giving the nod to Santes Creus.

The community fared no better than Poblet in the period of the secularization laws in the nineteenth century and in 1835 the monks left Santes Creus, after which the ritual sacking of the monastery was inevitable. It was not until 1950 that the Trust established to restore the main buildings was able to begin reconstruction and today the dormitory, cloister, church, courtyards and other corners can all be visited and enjoyed.

In summer concerts are held in the dormitory, a wonderful Early-Gothic, arched hall, which must be a notable experience for the music lover in such an historical milieu. At the end of your tour of the buildings you are shown a very effective *son-et-lumière* on the origins of the monastery and the daily lives of the monks, rounding-off what for most people are a few deeply satisfying hours in another world.

~ APPENDIX I ~

Dictionary of dishes described

Catalan	Spanish	English
Amanida d'enciams de sucre, sardina i ceba tendra i vinagreta d'all	Ensalada de lechuga, sardina y cebollas tiernas en una vinagreta de ajo	Lettuce salad with sardines and tender onions in a garlic vinaigrette
Amanida de bolets amb confit de pollastre i daus de formatge	Ensalada de setas con puré de pollo y dados de queso	Wild mushroom salad with a purée of chicken & small cheese 'dice'
Amanida de Xixoes	Ensalada de chicoes	Xixoes salad
Anchoves de l'Escala	Anchoas de l'Escala	Anchovies from l'Escala
Ànec amb figues	Pato con higos	Duck with figs
Ànec amb peres	Pato con peras	Duck with pears
Arrós a la cassola amb marisc o carn, tomaquet i verdures	Arroz a la cazuela con marisco o carne, tomate y verduras	Rice with shellfish or meat, tomato and vegetables
Bacallà a la graella amb all-i-oli	Bacalao a la pancha con all-i-oli	Grilled salt cod with all-i-oli
Bacallà amb cigrons, ovella i moro de porc	Bacalao con garbanzo, oerja y morro de cerdo	Salt cod with chickpeas, pig's ear and snout
Botifarra amb mongetes	Morcilla con judias	Catalan sausage with beans
Cabrit al forn	Cabrito asado	Roast kid
Calamar farcit	Calamar relleno	Stuffed squid
Calamarcets de costa a la plancha amb julibert	Calamarcitos de la costa a la plancha con perejil	Baby squid cooked on the grill with garlic and parsley
Calçots	Cebollitas a la parilla	Barbecued tender onions
Canalós	Canelones	Canneloni
Cargols	Caracoles	Snails
Carn a la pedra	Carne a la pizarra	Steak grilled on a hot slate
Carpaccio de pop amb manéc i vinagreta de llentilles	Carpaccio de pulpo con mango y vinagreta de lentejas	Carpaccio of octopus with mango and a lentil vinaigrette
Colomí	Pichón	Pigeon
Conill	Conejo	Rabbit
Crema catalana	Crema catalana	Light custard cream with caramel topping
Conill amb cigalas i cargols	Conejo con cigalas y caracoles	Rabbit with crayfish and snails
Crema freda de calabassó amb formatge fresc	Crems fría de calabacin con queso	Cold cream of courgette soup with cheese
Cua de bou guisada amb olives	Cola de buey con aceitunas	Oxtail with olives
Enciam templada de pedrer d'ànec i gambetes	Enslada templada de mollejas de pato y gambas	Warm salad of diced duck sweetbreads and prawns
Entrecot amb romaní	Entrecote con romero	Entrecôte with rosemary

172

Dictionary of dishes described – *(continued)*

Escalivada	Escalibada	Grilled and peeled peppers, aubergines and onions
Escudella	Cocido	Broth
Espinacs a la catalana	Espinacas a la catalana	Spinach Catalan style
Esqueixada de bacallà	Ensalada de bacalao frío con tomate	Raw salt cod served with tomatoes, onions and oil
Estofat de porc senglar	Estofado de jabalí	Stew of wild boar
Faves tendres guisades a la catalana	Habas tiernas guisadas a la catalana	Tender broad beans cooked Catalan style
Filets de cuixa de xai al forn amb patatas	Filetes de pierna de cordero con patatas	Fillets of leg of lamb with potatoes
Flam	Flan	Cream caramel
Gall del Penedès a l'ametlla	Pollo del Penedès con almendras	Penedès chicken with almonds
Gall del Penedès amb champinyons	Pollo del Penedès con champiñones	Penedès chicken with mushrooms
Gall tendre en vinagreta d'all	Pollo tierno en una vinagreta de ajo	Tender chicken in a garlic vinaigrette
Garrí ascit	Cochinillo	Roast suckling pig
Llebre amb mongetes, espàrrecs i rossinyols	Liebre con judías, espárragos y setas	Hare with beans, asparagus and wild mushrooms
Llum	Merluza	Hake
Mandonguilles amb gambetes	Albóndigas con gambas	Meat balls with prawns
Pechuga d'ànec amb mel	Pechuga de pato con miel	Breast of duck with honey
Pèsols amb botifarra	Guisantes con morcilla	Petits pois with Catalan sausage
Peus de porc amb cargòls	Pies de cerdo con caracoles	Pig's trotters with snails
Pollastre	Pollo	Chicken
Ravioli de cranca amb cervell de xai i salsa de bolets	Raviolis de centollo con sesos de cordero	Spider crab ravioli with mango and sheep's brains
Suquet de peix	Pescado en salsa con patatas	Fish stew
Suquet de raya amb gambas	Raya en salsa con gambas y patatas	Fish stew with ray and prawns
Tonyina fresca	Atún fresco	Fresh tunny fish
Truita ce riu	Trucha	River trout
Vedella amb bolets	Ternera con setas	Veal with a sauce of wild mushrooms
Xai a forn amb herbes de muntanya	Cordero asado con hierbas de montaña	Roast lamb seasoned with mountain herbs

173

Green Fees 1999

Note: all prices in Pesetas

Club	w/d (*) greenfees	w/e (*) greenfees	H'cap limit	Buggy	Indiv. 3 wheeler	Phone	Fax
Bonmont Terres Noves C.G.	5,000	7,000	no	5,000	2500	977-818140	977-818146
Cerdaña R.C.G.	5,000	7,000	no	5,000	no	972-141408	972-881338
Costa Brava C.G.	5,500	7,500	no	5,000	no	972-837005	972-837272
Costa Dorada C.G.	5,000[1]	10,000	no	4,000	no	977-653361	977-653028
D'Aro C.G.	5,500	8,000	no	4,500	no	972-826900	972-826906
El Prat R.C.G.	12,135	24,335	no	4,035	1515	93-3790278	93-3705102
Empordà G.C.	5,500	8,500	no	5,000	no	972-760450	972-757100
Fontanals de Cerdanya C.G.	5,000[3]	14,000	no	4,000	no	972-144374	972-890856
Girona C.G.	4,500	6,000	no	5,500	no	972-171641	972-171682
Llavaneres C.G.	6,000	12,000	no	4,000	no	93-7926050	93-7952558
Masia Bach C.G.	6,000	20,000	no	Note[2]	no	93-7726310	93-7726356
Osona-Montanya-El Brull C.G.	4,400	12,500	no	5,000	no	93-8840170	93-8840407
Pals C.G.	6,000	10,000	m=27; l=35	5,000	no	972-636006	972-637009
Peralada C.G.	6,000	7,500	no	5,000	no	972-538287	972-538236
Reus Aiguesverds C.G.	5,500	8,000	no	5,000	no	977-752725	977-751938
Sant Cugat C.G.	9,000	20,000	no	4,000	no	93-6743908	93-6755152
Terramar C.G.	5,800	8,900	no	4,300	no	93-8940580	93-8947051
Vallromanes C.G.	6,000	12,000	m=26; l=34	3,500	2000	93-5729064	93-5729330

Notes: w/d = weekdays; w/e = weekends
(1) 1 July to 15 September: Pts 8,000
(2) Included in greenfee if two people play
(3) August: Pts 14,000

Hotels and Restaurants

Hotels (H) Restaurants (R)

Location	Name	Phone
Arenys de Mar	El Bar del Puerto. R.	93-7921483
Barcelona	Can Ramonet. R.	93-3193064
Barcelona	Planet Hollywood. R.	93-2211111
Barcelona	Hard Rock Cafe. R.	93-2702305
Barcelona	Dive. R.	93-2258158
Barcelona	Los Caracoles. R.	93-3023185
Barcelona	Siete Puertas. R.	93-3193033
Barcelona	Agut d'Avingon. R.	93-3026034
Barcelona	Senyor Parellada. R.	93-3105094
Barcelona	Tragaluz. R.	93-4870621
Barcelona	4 Gats. R.	93-3024140
Barcelona	Hotel Jardí. H.	93-3015900
Bolvir	Torre del Remei. H&R.	972-140182
Breda	El Montseny. R.	93-870004
Breda	El Romaní. R.	972-871051
Club de Golf Terramar	Club Restaurant. R.	93-8940580
El Brull	El Castell. R.	93-8840063
El Brull	Can Pascual. R.	93-8840236
Granollers	La Fonda Europa. H&R.	93-8700312
La Costa del Montseny. R.	La Costa del Montseny. R.	93-8475251
Les Meranges	Can Borell. H&R.	972-880033
Llivia	Hotel Llivia. H.	972-146000
Llivia	Can Ventura. R.	972-896178
Martinet de Cerdanya	Hotel Boix. H&R.	973-515050
Montanya	Hotel Montanya. H.	93-8840606
Pals	Hotel de la Costa. H.	972-667700
Peralada	Mas Molí. R.	972-538281

Real Club de Golf La Cerdaña	Club Restaurant. R.	972-141408
Sant Felíu de Guíxols	La Gavina. H.	972-3211 00
Sant Felíu de Guíxols	El Dorado Petit. R.	972-321818
Sant Felíu de Guíxols	Can Toni. R.	972-321 026
Santa Cristina de Aro	Les Panolles. R.	972-837011
Tarragona	La Rambla. R.	977-238729
Tarragona	El Rebost. R.	977-231669
Tarragona	Restauarante Merlot. R	977-220652
Torrent (Pals)	Mas de Torrent. H&R.	972-303292
Vic	La Taula. R.	93-8863220
Vic	Basset. R.	93-8890212
Vic	Ca l'U. R.	93-8890345
Vilafranca del Penedès	Airolo. R.	93-8910365

Bibliography

Catalunya by Josep Pla, published by Ediciones Destino
Poblet by Josep Pla, published by Publicaciones de l'Abadia de Poblet
Salvador Dalí by Josep Pla, published by Dasa Edicions S.A.
Guia del Viajero - Espacios naturales de Catalunya, published by Susaeta Ediciones
Barcelona by Robert Hughes, published by Harvill Harper Collins
404 Spanish wines by Frank Snell, published by Lookout Publications S.A.
Sant Miguel del Fay, mil años de historia, by A. Pladevall, published by Bergas Industrias Gráficas
Catalunya y sus comarcas by Jaime Bover Argerich, published by Fondo cultural de Ia Caja de Ahorros Provincial de la Diputación de Barcelona
Les Comarques de Catalunya, published by Editor Dissenys Culturals S.L.
Diccionari Nomenclator de Pobles i Poblats de Catalunya, published by Editorial Aedos, Barcelona
Lleida by lgnacio Gonzalez Orozco, published by Guias Azules de Espana S.A.
Dalí... Dalí... Dalí by Max Gérard, published by Editorial Blume
Gent Nostra - Dalí by Jaume Socias, published by Edicions de Nou Art Thor
Salvador Dalí by Conroy Maddox, published by Benedict Taschen Verlag GMBH
The Life and Works of Dalí by Nathaniel Harris, published by Parragon Book Service Ltd.
El Barrio Gótico de Barcelona by Aurelio Díez Aparicio, published by Editorial Everest S.A.
El Baix Empordà by Albert Arbós, published by Dissenys Culturals
Peralada by Miguel Golobardes Vila, published by Ediciones Palacio Peralada

El Gironès by Enric Mirambell, published by Dissenys Culturals S.L.

Barcelona (various contributors), published by El Pais Aguilar

El Templo de la Sagrada Familia by Josep Maria Carandel, published by Triangle Postals S.L.

Catalunya sobre Ruedas, series published by La Vanguardia newspaper

Catalunya Verda, series published by La Vanguardia newspaper

Curso de Vinos Españoles, published by Vinoselección

Catalunya Universal (various contributors), published by La Vanguardia newspaper

El Garraf, by Josep Maria Ràfols, published by Generalitat de Catalunya

El Tarragonès by Francesc Roig, published by Dessenys Culturals S.L.